AND THEN THERE WAS:

—The man in England who conned people in bars into buying him drinks by claiming to have terminal cancer, and died when his story convinced one man to end his suffering by suffocating him with a pillow.

—The Colorado man who drank a case of beer to get the nerve to break into a store, then tried to pry open the front door with a crowbar. When he saw people inside staring at him, he realized the store was open.

—The New Englander charged with unlawful possession of a rodent when he was caught driving with a live gray squirrel tied to his windshield wiper.

—The Rhode Island woman who won $14.7 million in a lottery, only to be convicted of welfare fraud.

—The Texas lawyer who requested that only jurors less than five feet tall be chosen.

Being dumb may not be a crime—but it can be criminally funny, as you will discover in the 460 side-splitting but absolutely authentic stories straight from the pages of newspapers around the world in

LAW AND DISORDER
Weird News of Crime and Punishment

LAW
AND
DISORDER

WEIRD NEWS
OF CRIME
AND
PUNISHMENT

Compiled by Roland Sweet

A SIGNET BOOK

SIGNET
Published by the Penguin Group
Penguin Books USA Inc., 375 Hudson Street,
New York, New York 10014, U.S.A.
Penguin Books Ltd, 27 Wrights Lane,
London W8 5TZ, England
Penguin Books Australia Ltd, Ringwood,
Victoria, Australia
Penguin Books Canada Ltd, 10 Alcorn Avenue,
Toronto, Ontario, Canada M4V 3B2
Penguin Books (N.Z.) Ltd, 182–190 Wairau Road,
Auckland 10, New Zealand

Penguin Books Ltd, Registered Offices:
Harmondsworth, Middlesex, England

First published by Signet, an imprint of Dutton Signet,
a division of Penguin Books USA Inc.

First Printing, January, 1994
10 9 8 7 6 5 4 3 2 1

 REGISTERED TRADEMARK—MARCA REGISTRADA

Printed in the United States of America

To a T.
Treats & Trust

Acknowledgments

I'm indebted to the newspapers that first published these dispatches, and to the reporters and editors who gathered the facts from the police blotters of the world. Clippings for this volume came from Associated Press, Reuters, and United Press International wire services, and from the *Baltimore Sun & Evening Sun, Boston Globe, Chicago Tribune, Cleveland Plain Dealer, Columbus* (OH) *Dispatch, Denver Post, Fairfax* (VA) *Journal, Insight, International Herald Tribune, Knoxville* (TN) *News-Sentinel, Los Angeles Times, Miami Herald, Minneapolis Star-Tribune, New Orleans Times-Picayune, New York Post, New York Times, Newark* (NJ) *Star-Ledger, Newsweek, Philadelphia Inquirer, Rocky Mountain News, San Francisco Chronicle, Syracuse* (NY) *Herald-Journal & Post-Standard, USA Today, Washington Post, Washington Times,* and *World Press Review.*

Thanks, also, to Mike Greenstein, Steve Moss, Dick Wien, Kihm Winship, Rick Mariani, Jim Turosak, D. Kingsley Hahn, Margaret Engle, Kathy Cashell, Kelley Culmer, Gail Ross, and Ed Stackler.

Special thanks to John Kohut and Chuck Shepherd.

Contents

Introduction

Crooks get caught not because crime doesn't pay. They get caught because crooks are boneheads.

The criminal mastermind of detective novels is fiction. The fact is that no burglar has ever won the Nobel Prize for Not Bungling.

Nor are crime fighters ideal candidates for Mensa, the high-IQ club. Newspapers teem with tales of incompetent cops, lame-brained lawyers, and injudicious judges.

This book contains some 450 news stories that I've gleaned from the daily papers. They recount odd crimes and odder crooks, bad good guys, ridiculous lawsuits, courtroom antics, weird weapons, and even hapless victims (proving there's no such thing as an innocent bystander!). What makes them so unbelievable is that every one of them is true.

All are presented without embellishment or commentary. I've made no effort to follow up on them, beyond reading the paper to make sure accounts were not retracted, challenged, or contradicted. I've included names for authenticity, even though a few of the original suspects may have since been released, had the charges changed or dropped, or been acquitted. These items are presented not as news, but as having *been* news—that is, history. Taken together, they prove that crooks, cops, and convicts do the dumbest things. And very often the funniest.

Roland Sweet
Mount Vernon, Virginia

Crooks Too Stupid To Break The Law

Incompetency isn't against the law, but some law-breakers should be allowed to plead not guilty by reason of stupidity. These are the bank robbers who write their holdup notes on the back of deposit slips with their names and addresses on the other side, or the robbers who can't even manage a decent getaway. Cases fall into two categories: "Mensa Rejects" (crooks too stupid to pull it off) and "Got Caught Stupid" (crooks who pulled it off—up to a point).

Mensa Rejects

Michael Coleman, 26, borrowed a pencil from a customer waiting to use an automatic teller machine outside a London bank, then used the ATM as a desk to write out a holdup note. He stopped writing occasionally to ask the customer for help with spelling while other people waited in line to use the machine.

Once inside the bank, Coleman pulled out a plastic pistol and put strips of tape on his face

1

as a disguise. Then he got in the line for a teller. While he was waiting, a customer grabbed him and shouted for help. Coleman panicked, seized $340 from another customer, and fled.

Outside the bank, he dropped a knife with a clean set of fingerprints. He also left his prints on his getaway bicycle before abandoning it. Prosecutor Linda Stern told a court that Coleman "is probably one of the most inept and amateurish bank robbers on record." He pleaded guilty as charged.

Shortly after eight o'clock one morning, two men ran toward a bank in suburban Washington waving guns and wearing bandanas over their faces. According to Arlington County, VA, police, the first man ran full speed into the door, only to find it locked. As he hit the door, the second man ran into him, and both slammed into the door. "They hit it really hard and bounced back," said bank manager Dwight Smith, who had just locked the door behind him after entering the bank.

The two staggered back to their getaway van. It wouldn't start at first, and once they did get it running, it sputtered for several blocks, forcing them to abandon it and flee on foot.

☡

A gang of 10 masked men stormed the central post office in Bologna, Italy, held the staff and customers at gunpoint, then detonated a charge in front of a vault containing $500,000 in pension payments that had just been delivered. They misjudged the strength of the explosive device, however, and 45 people were injured by flying glass, furniture, and parts of the masonry ceiling, which came crashing down on top of the safe, forcing the gang to leave most of the money behind.

New York City police had no trouble identifying three men who shot up a Harlem bar, killing three patrons. They left behind Polaroid photos of themselves posing with their guns, which were taken by a street photographer in the bar just before they fired 15 shots into the crowd of 40 to 50 people, some of whom identified the men from the snapshots.

⚖

J. Douglas Creswell was sentenced to 25 years in prison for attempting to rob a motel in DeRidder, LA. The holdup failed after Creswell, as he entered the motel lobby with knife in hand, pulled a plastic garbage bag over his head so he wouldn't be recognized. He then realized he had forgotten to cut eyeholes in the bag. He asked the clerk for money anyway, but she refused and he left.

When a gunman tried to rob a Fort Worth, TX, gas station, night shift clerk Judy Frisco, 39, sat calmly in her bulletproof glass cashier's cage and phoned the police, ignoring the would-be robber's threats to "blow this window away." According to police, the man "apparently became weary from the neglect" and fled.

A tall, burly man entered a San Francisco liquor store, pointed a revolver at clerk Frank Boutte, and demanded money. According to police, when Boutte refused, "the suspect then began to cry," put his gun in his pocket, and ran out of the store.

Three teenagers in Syracuse, NY, who admitted stealing 100,000 baseball cards valued at $20,000, explained that they traded them for 11,000 new basketball cards worth about $280.

Shortly after the breakup of the Soviet Union, five men tried to hold up a bank in Baku, Azerbaijan. The bank staff obligingly opened the safes to show them rows of bare shelves. "The raiders were let down by their ignorance of the state the republic's finances are in," Russian radio reported. "No money has come into any of the banks in Baku for the last two months."

When a man pulled two guns on Houston convenience store clerk Wazir Jiwi and demanded money, Jiwi asked how much he wanted for one of the guns. The man said $100, which Jiwi paid him.

Then Jiwi offered to buy the second gun. The robber handed it over, grabbed the cash, and headed for the exit.

Meanwhile, Jiwi had pushed a button under the counter that automatically locked the door. "He turned to me and asked what was going on," Jiwi said. "I told him to bring the money back and I would let him go. He brought the money back, and I opened the door."

Two gunmen looking for a target among the fashionable jewelry stores on San Francisco's Post Street burst into Ciro, which sells low-priced costume jewelry. "The robber told me to fill up the bag with jewelry, and I asked him, 'Why?'" said clerk Cy Homitz. "I told him, 'It isn't real.' He seemed surprised and said, 'Oh.'"

5

Unconvincing Explanations

When police in Glendale Heights, IL, arrested Eric A. Hoyt, 21, and Peter A. Thordason, 25, after catching them taking a Christmas tree from a grocery store lot, Thordason explained to the officers that he and his friend weren't stealing the tree. They just wanted to see how long it would take Thordason to run around the building carrying the tree while Hoyt timed him.

When police in Elkton, MD, arrested Henry E. Hamilton for robbing a bank after they found the loot in his home the next day, Hamilton explained that he got the money from a man he met at a shopping center who offered him $5,000 if he would hold on to it awhile.

San Francisco police questioned Jesse J. "Al" King, 54, after a shopper at a downtown department store told a security guard that King was writing a holdup note. King, whose bank robbery convictions date back to 1980, admitted writing the note ("This is a stickup. Give $50,000. I have a gun and will kill you if you do not get me 50"). But he explained he only wrote it to include in a book he was writing on robbing banks.

Got Caught Stupid

Three men planning to steal art treasures from Britain's National Gallery found the wheels of their getaway car had been booted because it was illegally parked. Since none of the three had enough cash to pay the fine to have the clamp removed, they jacked up the car and tried to remove it themselves. Police spotted them and found suspicious items in their car, including two hand grenades and a plan of the gallery with a mark signaling a room containing Van Gogh paintings worth $240,000.

A couple charged with stealing film from a drugstore in Merchantville, NJ, made a clean getaway, but they forgot to take their six-year-old son with them. Police Chief Robert Ward explained, "He gave their names and the school that he attended."

A woman suspected of shoplifting in Chapel Hill, NC, ran from the store when an employee approached her. Police were able to track her down and charge her with larceny because when she fled she left behind a stroller containing her 14-month-old son.

Police investigating a convenience store holdup in Portland, OR, had little trouble locating suspect Clarence Craig Anderson, 39. They said he had been in such a hurry to make his getaway that he left his dog behind, tied up outside the store. Police looked at the dog's tags and found Anderson's name and address.

After robbing a restaurant in Buena Park, CA, a 38-year-old man was in such a hurry to get away before his victims saw his license plate number that he began pulling out of the parking lot without his girlfriend, who had been waiting outside. "The girl was hollering after him and slapping the back of the car," said the restaurant's owner, Larry Anderson.

Anderson said the robber left, then doubled back for his girlfriend and sped off. Police caught up with them after a blowout forced the couple to abandon the car. "I guess he didn't want to leave me," Nancy Horton, 33, said after their arrest. "He came back for me, but it didn't work out."

A front-page photograph in the Kansas City (MO) *Times* showed a man loading pumpkins at a farm in Leavenworth County. The caption identified him as Bud Bradbury, but FBI agents recognized him as Everett D. Bradbury, who was wanted for failing to appear at a probation hearing in connection with his conviction for theft. They went to the farm to arrest him. "I think the agents were amazed that this person was on the front page of the *Times*, along with his name," says FBI spokesperson Ben Berry.

After President Bush's second State of the Union address, Pittsburgh television station KDKA interviewed James Schlagel, 33, at a local cafe for his reaction to the speech. Schlagel waved a small American flag and said the country should support "President Reagan." Federal and city law-enforcement agents watching the newscast recognized Schlagel as the man they said stole a police cruiser from a shopping center a month earlier, rammed two other police cars, and fled. Within minutes, they descended on the tavern and arrested the suspect.

When New York police began chasing two robbery suspects, one of them jumped over a spiked fence surrounding a Harlem police station. "I was thinking, this guy is nuts," said Joe Doyle, one of the pursuing officers, who yelled for assistance. Officers rushing out of the station found the suspect hanging upside down by his pants, which were around his ankles and stuck on the fence spikes.

In Syracuse, NY, the driver of a stolen car led police on a twenty-eight-minute chase. Police had no problem following the car because the driver signaled every move he made. "At every turn, we knew exactly where he was going," Investigator Gerard Verrillo said.

A man tried to rob a store in Columbia, MO, with a knife, but the store happened to be a gun shop. Well-armed employees thwarted the attempt.

In Pensacola, FL, police officer Dusty Cutler was chasing a man dressed as a woman, who was suspected of stealing women's clothing from a store. The suspect's underwear, which was stuffed with the stolen items, dropped to his ankles and tripped him. He pulled off the undies and continued running, throwing more clothing from his purse. Cutler finally caught and arrested him.

Police in New York City didn't have any trouble locating a prisoner who escaped from the hospital while awaiting trial for grand larceny. They nabbed him riding the subway—still wearing his hospital gown with an IV attached to his arm.

Marcy Sanders, who tried to extort $2 million by claiming to have hidden bombs in airport terminals at Charleston and Columbia, SC, wouldn't agree to a police suggestion that he meet face to face with the police to get his money. Instead, Sanders told police to deposit the money directly, giving the name of his bank and his account number.

Richard Brown of Boston stopped a police cruiser to report a fire in a nearby variety store. Rather than thank the dutiful citizen, the officers arrested him for starting the fire himself, since Brown was carrying four gallons of gasoline and an unused firebomb.

⚖

Steven Little drank a case of beer before getting up enough nerve to break into a store in Longmont, CO. He was trying to pry open the front door with a crowbar when he saw people inside staring at him and realized that the store was still open.

Police in Morlaix, France, arrested a burglar with a habit of eating snacks in the kitchens of homes he broke into. They identified him from dental records after he left behind his false teeth at one home.

⚖

In Baltimore, Bernard Campbell, 19, was arrested for the murder of a local stickup artist, Willie "Peepsight" Chambers, 37. While two police detectives drove him from the jail to the courthouse for a bail hearing, they began discussing how whoever shot Chambers did them a favor. Finally, one cop said he'd like to shake the hand of the killer. Campbell shoved his cuffed hands forward to shake the officer's hand. After realizing what he had done, Campbell pleaded guilty.

Denver police arrested Lawrence VanCleave, 26, for attempted burglary when they found him, wearing nothing but his socks, stuck in the kitchen vent of the Valley Cafe. According to Detective Ralph Bravo, an employee who arrived at 5 a.m. heard a man shouting, "Help me, help me," and called 911. When police arrived, they found the 6-foot-2, 175-pound VanCleave wedged in the 14-inch-diameter pipe. His arms were on the roof near his clothes, his torso was trapped in the pipe, and his legs dangled from the ceiling opening. Noting that VanCleave had been stuck that way for about five hours, Bravo said rescuers had to spray WD-40 lubricant into the vent, then pull the nude suspect back to the roof.

A man who Chicago police say tried to break into a Chinese restaurant through a ceiling vent took off his clothes to make his entry easier but got stuck anyway and died from exposure. Ser-

geant Mike McComb said the man was trapped
in 5-degree weather for about 10 hours.

In Houston, Lawrence Nicholas Sanson pleaded
guilty to breaking into a liquor store and downing a $67 jug of Dom Perignon. Sanson was
caught while making his getaway when he got
stuck in the ceiling and had to call out to police
to rescue him.

⚖

After setting off an alarm while burglarizing a
sporting goods store in Silver Spring, MD, an
18-year-old man hid in an air duct. He waited
there for more than 36 hours before deciding it
was safe to make his getaway. But when he
looked to make sure the police were gone, they
weren't—and they arrested him.

Two teenagers who robbed a bank in Des
Moines, WA, of $960 returned to their getaway
car to find it had a dead battery. When they got
out to check under the hood, they locked their
keys and the loot in the car. Fleeing on foot,
they ran straight to the car driven by a police
detective dispatched to the bank.

"This was a bungled job from start to finish,"
Sergeant Mitch Barker said. "All we needed was
Curly. We had Larry and Moe."

An 18-year-old man attempting to rob a convenience store in Hutchinson, KS, stabbed himself in the face while cutting the power cord of the cash register. He fled with the cash register but dropped it outside the store. Passersby chased him into an alley, where police arrested him.

FBI agents investigating a bank robbery in St. Paul, MN, tracked the suspect to a bar four blocks away. When they showed a bar employee a bank surveillance photograph, she not only recognized the man as a regular customer but pointed him out as he sat at the bar. After the agents arrested Franklin D. Kirk, 49, they searched his apartment and found half of a torn document from his probation office. The other half had already turned up at the bank with the holdup note written on the back.

In Salem, MA, burglars trying to break into a store vault with a welding torch had to flee empty handed after they accidentally ignited stacks of money. The fire activated a smoke alarm that summoned firefighters and police.

Knox County, TN, sheriff's deputies arrested Steven Clift Preston, 21, for attempted burglary after

th and
ness

they found him stuck in the sliding glass door of a home. The door, wedged shut with a piece of wood, had been pushed open a few inches and Preston, who was described as very skinny, apparently tried to squeeze through. Reported Deputy Jim Neubert, "He couldn't get in or out."

Police in London were able to catch a gang robbing a mortgage loan company because the gang's lookout, Brian Scarborough, left his glasses at home. Police explained that Scarborough was worried the frames were too distinctive and that he might be identified. But without them he was unable to spot police officers who arrived during the holdup.

St. Paul, MN, police charged Glenn M. Peterson, 29, with breaking into a public library. They said he apparently tried to break open a coin-operated copier's money box by shoving the machine downstairs. But all that did was get black copy toner on the floor, where Peterson stepped in it. Police found him a few blocks away after following the trail of footprints and feathers from his down-filled jacket, which had been sliced open by jagged glass while he was breaking into the library.

In Syracuse, NY, Richard H. Stowell, 27, who was on parole after serving time for a bank robbery in which he was captured while trying to make his getaway by bus, was charged with robbing another bank and, once again, trying to escape on a city bus.

Kevin Kayrouz, 22, applied for a job with the Johnson County, IN, sheriff's department, but he wound up behind bars when a computer background check found he was wanted on charges of forgery and receiving stolen property.

⚖

When Margaret Scherer, 88, pulled her car over to ask directions in Deerfield Beach, FL, a 31-year-old woman reached into her car and grabbed a bank envelope. According to Broward County sheriff's deputy Don Devine, two teenagers promptly grabbed the money from the thief and ran off, prompting the woman to yell and attract a crowd. When police arrived, the thief identified the teens and police arrested all three.

San Antonio, TX, police investigating a liquor store burglary found no shortage of evidence pointing to Carlos Carrasco, 24. When he broke through the roof of the store, he cut his hand on a jagged metal edge. Once inside, he tried to toss a bottle of whiskey through the hole, but he missed and it crashed to the floor, setting off the burglar alarm.

Carrasco tried to escape by climbing out through the hole, but he slipped and fell on the broken whiskey bottle, slashing his arm and leg. When he did manage to get outside, he fell off the roof and his wallet popped out of his pocket for police to find, along with a trail of blood that they followed to his home.

When they found an unpublished novel that he had written about a firefighter who torches buildings, authorities charged Captain John L. Orr, 42, a chief arson investigator for the Glendale, CA, fire department, with deliberately setting fire to three businesses. After showing the judge a letter from Orr to a publisher, describing his novel, *Points of Origin,* as "a fact-based work that follows the pattern of an actual arsonist that has been setting serial fires in California over the past eight years," federal prosecutors announced they also suspected Orr of starting at least a dozen other fires in central California over a two-year period whenever he was in the region to attend arson conferences.

In Barcelona, Spain, ex-convict Bernardino "El Nino" Ballester, 28, went on a live television talk show to tell about his years behind bars. He praised the prison system and spoke so movingly about his problems caring for his wife and child that some viewers called the station to offer jobs and cash. Others called the police, however, and identified Ballester as the armed man who robbed a jewelry shop of $200,000 in gems and pistol-whipped the shop owner. Ballester was arrested leaving the TV studio.

Federal authorities in Madison, WI, arrested a 26-year-old man for counterfeiting, after clerks at a printing-supply store notified them that a customer had been holding dollar bills up to a color chart before ordering a particular shade of green ink.

A bank robber in St. Leonards, Australia, leaned over the teller's counter to check the cash drawer at the same time the teller activated a bulletproof screen. It rose from the counter, pinning the robber's head between it and the frame of the teller's cage, crushing the robber to death.

Robert Laughton broke into Rick's Liquor store in Los Angeles by climbing onto the roof, cutting through an air-conditioning vent, squeezing through the 2-foot opening, and dropping 10 feet into the store. When his landing set off the store's motion-sensing alarm, however, he tried to escape but found that he was unable to climb back up to reach his entry hole, and that all the doors and windows were locked and barred.

According to police Sergeant Roger Ferguson,

after Laughton "came to the horrible conclusion that he could not get out," he phoned the police to come rescue him. Police were unable to get him out to arrest him, so they told him to poke around for something to help him reach the hole. Just 15 feet away, he found a ladder, which he used to climb out through the roof to the waiting officers.

In Long Beach, CA, the wife of police Sergeant Danny Holland reported a pair of $200 earrings was missing from her home. Suspecting a woman who had been installing drywall in the home, Holland called her to the police station. "She was wearing the earrings when she showed up for questioning," Captain Art Roberts said. "That was another brilliant move."

⚖

Police in Haverhill, MA, identified Richard C. Gillis, 44, as their chief suspect in a bank robbery, after finding his name and address written on the deposit slip the robber used for his holdup note. Even the handwriting was the same. They arrested Gillis a few minutes after the robbery when they found him struggling to make his getaway on a bicycle. He was covered with red dye, coughing and sneezing, and trailing smoke from the exploding dye pack that the teller had hidden in the bundles of money.

Police in Greensburg, PA, arrested Adam P. Walton, 18, after they stopped him for a traffic violation and found $1,500 worth of stolen electronics equipment in his car. They also found a home-made music video of Walton rapping about how he "pulled down a wall" to enter a store and steal the equipment he used for his recording. Walton denied that his video rap referred to the robbery police charged him with, even though they said the break-in involved removing a wooden wall panel on the store's garage.

Sacramento, CA, police, responding to a bank robbery at the American Savings Bank, found suspect Ed Rose, 55, standing outside the bank waiting for his getaway car. The driver, Theodore Kuhl, 35, had taken it to be washed.

In Rock Springs, WY, John Stephens, 17, was on a bicycle, making his getaway from a burglary. According to Sheriff Gary Bailiff, the youth dropped his gun, stopped to pick it up, shoved it back in his belt, and accidentally shot himself dead.

After robbing a woman in Baltimore, an armed man in his early twenties was putting the .22-

20

caliber semiautomatic pistol in his waistband when the weapon fired, hitting him in the groin and causing him to bleed to death.

Police in Olathe, KS, arrested an 18-year-old Texas man for robbing a fast-food restaurant while wearing a George Bush mask. After the holdup, the robber's car wouldn't start in the 2-degree weather, so he came back inside to ask the restaurant manager for a jump-start. Summoned by a computer alarm that the manager had triggered before the robber returned, police found him in the parking lot trying to get the car started.

Soon after Ronald Gatson, 27, was released from prison, where he'd spent four years for breaking into a garage and trying to steal a snowblower, he was arrested for breaking into 76 garages in Milwaukee and stealing 15 more snowblowers.

In Hartford, CT, a man broke into an apartment by knocking down the front door. The noise woke the two men inside, who happened to be police officers. They arrested the 30-year-old suspect.

Four thieves broke into a van at a parking lot in Lakeland, FL, in December 1990. But before they could make their getaway, three police officers hiding in the back arrested them. The thieves had broken into a van being used by a special unit dispatched to combat parking-lot crime.

A similar case occurred two weeks earlier in La Habra, CA. Two men tried to break into a van being used for surveillance by undercover police. "We just sat there while they tried to get in," said Investigator Rich Cook. "They tried three times." The officers radioed for a marked patrol car to arrest the men, but the thieves saw it. Before they could flee, however, the officers in the van jumped out and arrested them.

The Fickle Finger of Fate

Mark McKenna, 21, admitted in London's Central Criminal Court that he tried to rob a betting shop by sticking his fingers under his sweater to look like a gun. He was caught when, as a cashier handed over $325, McKenna absentmindedly pulled out his hand to take it.

Authorities investigating a wrecked mailbox in Hays, KS, had no trouble identifying the vandals. One of them left behind not just a fingerprint but the finger itself. Ellis County sheriff's deputy Dave Zellmer said that after the driver of a pickup truck ran over the mailbox, it got hung up underneath the truck. While the driver rocked the truck back and forth, the passenger got out, reached underneath, and tried to loosen the mailbox. In the process, part of his thumb was severed. Zell-mer checked local emergency rooms for some-one who had been treated for a torn-off thumb and arrested Stephen Lantz, 27, who identified the driver.

New York City police arrested Paul Miller, 20, when he sought medical attention for his bleeding hand. He and two other men had re-portedly entered a Brooklyn fast-food restau-rant, taken $600 from the cash registers, and turned to flee. A shotgun that Miller had been holding went off, severing the ring finger from his left hand. As he bent to pick it up, he spot-ted a wallet that a patron had hastily thrown to the floor when he saw the robbery. Miller decided to leave the finger and take the wallet, which contained $4.50.

Dallas police charged James Carol Grisby with a department store burglary after finding part of a finger in a shoebox, making a fingerprint from it, and matching the print to Grisby. Grisby explained that he had accidentally cut off the finger while entering the store through a broken window.

Police in Reading, England, charged Clive McGee with the shooting death of a robbery victim. They said that when McGee shot the victim, he also shot off his own index finger. Police found it next to the corpse and arrested McGee when he went to a hospital to have his injured hand treated.

When the kidnappers of Michael Varone, 25, of Peterborough, England, called his parents seeking $10,000 ransom, Nick and Marguerita Varone said they would need time to raise the money. The kidnappers agreed and said they would speak to them later from the same public phone. Then they gave the Varones the number. "We won't call," they said. "You ring us."

The Varones immediately called the police, who traced the location of the pay phone and arrested two suspects who showed up at the appointed time. After recovering Michael Varone, Chief Constable Keith Povey observed, "The kidnap was perhaps not as sophisticated as one might have expected or feared."

A thief who broke into the apartment of Houston Rockets basketball player Chuck Nevitt in 1990 and stole a championship ring was arrested after he called the Rockets office to ask how much the ring was worth. He left his telephone number for someone to call him back with the figure.

Christopher Kerns, 18, was arrested in Bangor, MN, for stealing 30 checks and cashing some over a week's time at a Casco Northern Bank automatic teller machine. According to a sheriff's official, Kerns had gotten more than $2,000 before he was caught when he went inside the bank and complained angrily that he deposited a check for $700, but the machine would give him only $200. An employee explained that Kerns would have to wait until the check cleared.

The next day, authorities said, Kerns tried the machine again, but this time it kept his card. He went into the bank to get it back. Instead, suspicious bank officials notified the authorities.

A man who robbed a Birmingham, England, post office was leaving the building when his accomplice ran him down with their getaway motorcycle. In the ensuing confusion, the bandits dropped the stolen security box, which contained $28,000. An antitheft device went off, spraying the bank notes and the two men with a bright red dye. They left the money but managed to escape by flagging down a woman motorist and stealing her car.

⚖

During an interview for a job as a state trooper, Yvonne Adams, 20, of Columbus, OH, was asked if she had ever committed any indiscretions that would affect her performance as a law-enforcement officer. Yes, she admitted, she and her husband Raymond had stolen a new car the previous year. After the interview, Raymond Adams arrived in the stolen car to meet his wife. Both were arrested.

Arthur Gloria, 20, wanted to join the Chicago police force but had no way to get to the entrance exam location. So he accepted a friend's offer to lend him a stolen car. He parked the car illegally, blocking a crosswalk at an intersection near the test site and attracting the attention of police. They ran a check of the license plate and found that the car was stolen. They arrested Gloria after he returned to the car and started it up with a screwdriver.

In Jacksonville, FL, a man tried to rob a supermarket wearing a paper bag over his head. The bag, which had eyeholes cut in it so the robber could see, shifted during the holdup. When he moved it back into place, it ripped, exposing the face of a regular customer. "I yelled, 'Bob!' " said clerk Keetek Dore. "Then he ran away." Police said they didn't know if Bob was armed because he was wearing a paper bag over his hand, too.

A St. Paul, MN, shoplifting suspect trying to elude two security guards ducked into a lobby— of the police station. He attracted the attention of the officer manning the lobby because he was wearing an extra pair of pants. The officer added, "They had the price tag right on them."

Three burglars who broke into Penrose High School in Auckland, New Zealand, were nabbed in the act because they did not flee when they set off a burglar alarm. The three, who tried to make off with musical instruments, were deaf-mutes.

A passenger aboard a Greyhound bus on the New York State Thruway near Buffalo held up a package that he claimed was a bomb, announced a holdup, and ordered everyone off the bus. Driver Graham T. Dornford suggested that the robber get off first and everybody else would follow him. When the robber disembarked, Dornford drove off. The stranded man then robbed a nearby house but was nabbed by a neighbor who clubbed him with the butt of a shotgun.

In Mississippi, Jack Talley, 30, being sought for the stabbing deaths of his father, mother, and uncle, was arrested the day after the crime in a neighboring county when he tried to sell his broken-down car. "He was passing through and was having car trouble," Madison County investigator J. Ledbetter said. "He was talking to a group of folks, trying to sell it, when we approached him." Authorities noted that Talley was wearing bloodstained clothes, apparently the same ones he wore at the time of the murders.

In Frederikshavn, Denmark, a 23-year-old man sneaked into a camping couple's tent in the middle of the night and tried to rape the woman. The struggle woke the husband, who punched the attacker several times in the face and chased him off. The husband reported the incident to police, who apprehended the would-be rapist when he showed up at the police station to lodge a complaint against the husband for attacking him.

A 41-year-old man in Troy, MT, fell behind on his car payments, but figured to come out ahead by burying the car, reporting it stolen, and collecting the insurance. Police learned about the scheme, however, after the man bragged around town about his swindle.

John N. Dyson, 46, wanted for abducting his two adopted children from their home in England, took them to Prescott, AZ. Authorities there were ready to arrest him, but had to wait two months before they could complete the paperwork required in international cases. By that time, Dyson had fled with the children. He was located in Louisiana, however, after he dropped by the Kenner police station to report a stolen handbag and a routine computer check turned up his fugitive's warrant.

⚖

Billy Forrest, convicted of armed robbery and sentenced to serve 45 years, escaped from a minimum-security facility in Nashville, TN, in July 1980 and eluded authorities for 11½ years. He was recaptured in December 1991 in New York by transit police who caught him hopping a subway turnstile trying to beat the $1.15 fare. A background check turned up the outstanding warrant.

Michael Schinkel, 36, was arrested in 1991 for the 1986 death of his former girlfriend. Her partially decomposed body was found in a freezer left behind when Schinkel, his wife Renee, and their infant son were evicted from their home in Galt, CA, for not paying rent. The only witness at the preliminary hearing, sheriff's deputy Wayne Irey, testified that Schinkel had been telling people for years that he had a body locked in a freezer.

⚖

Mildred Juanita King Brooks, 57, of Baltimore, pleaded guilty to possession of cocaine with intent to distribute it, after she was caught trying to smuggle the drug into an awards banquet for recovering drug abusers at the Maryland Correctional Institution. The cocaine was found in five orange balloons that were wrapped in a handkerchief and stuffed in the woman's pantyhose.

In Gainesville, FL, a convicted burglar who told police he left his house-arrest program because he was bored was rearrested after a woman caught him inside her home playing Nintendo. Police also charged Kelly Lee Hardyman, 19, with breaking into another house earlier the same day and playing a Nintendo game there, too.

After robbing an armored car in upstate New York of nearly $3 million, Gary LaTray and Timothy DeMarc drove south but left a clear trail for the authorities. At their first stop, they hid $611,000 under a motel bed because they couldn't carry it, and they threw out thousands more at another stopover. Arriving in Washington, DC, they hired prostitutes; sipped champagne at a trendy nightclub; bought expensive clothes and jewelry; and cruised the streets in a 30-foot limousine with two color televisions, a VCR, and a bed. Six days after the robbery, FBI agents caught up with them in Virginia Beach, VA.

Not Necessarily Stupid (But Definitely Guilty)

Even the best-laid plans of the criminal mind go awry. The ways crooks get caught are endless, prompting more than one of them to mutter, "Curses, foiled again!"

Police in Brest, France, arrested Pierre Morvan, 26, who confessed to robbing and murdering farmer Jean Favennec, 86. A shop clerk tipped off the authorities after Morvan paid for some shoes. The wrinkled bills he handed her had a distinctive odor, and she recalled that Favennec was known for carrying his savings in his socks.

Wanted for murder and kidnapping, Jerry Barnes, 33, eluded authorities for a week before being shot to death in Hattiesburg, MS, by a 14-year-old boy while trying to steal a van belonging to the boy's family.

Moments after a man handed a San Francisco bank teller a note demanding money, a police officer thwarted his getaway by tackling him inside the bank. During the tussle, the officer noticed the suspect's white cane and realized he was blind. "I even had to ask somebody to lead me to the bank," Richard Dunbar, 34, said after his arrest. "If I got away with the money, I would have had to ask somebody for directions once I got outside."

A blind man handed a threatening note to a bank teller in Vallejo, CA, and collected $105. He was arrested after asking the teller to help him leave the building and she refused. Police Lieutenant Reginald Garcia reported that the first thing the 27-year-old suspect asked when he was apprehended was, "Are you the police?"

New York City police didn't have any trouble finding a suspect in the shooting of Howard Felix. While Felix was being treated for multiple gunshot wounds in the emergency room of Lincoln Hospital, another man who'd been shot was brought in and placed on the gurney next to him. Felix took one look at the second man and identified him as the man who shot him.

Arson investigators in Hermiston, OR, interrogated Richard Meacham and then left the room for a few minutes. When they returned, Meacham reportedly had set fire to his chair.

Police in Juneau, AK, arrested Ricky S. Sumdum, 31, for trying to break into a room at a hotel hosting a convention of Alaska police officers. In Sumdum's case, the intended victim was Brent Moody, police chief of Wrangell, who heard Sumdum prying open a window and grabbed his gun to greet him.

In Homewood, AL, two men burst into a motel room intending to rob the seven occupants, whom they had seen with a wad of money. The men turned out to be police officers setting up a drug sting. One of the robbers was armed and covered the officers while his accomplice started collecting their wallets.

"We had guns in our holsters, guns on shelves, guns everywhere, but we couldn't get to them," said one of the cops. Finally, one officer distracted the gunman while another eased his gun out of his holster and shot the man to death.

33

Police investigating a service station burglary in Whakatane, New Zealand, discovered that the security camera didn't reveal the burglar's face but it did capture the distinctive stripes of his underwear when he bent over to pick up some groceries he dropped. Police sergeant Tony Moller said that when officers questioned a suspect he denied the crime. Then they asked him to drop his trousers. When they told him that he was wearing the same underwear, he confessed.

Police were able to catch two men who they said held up a food market in Ordway, CO, after one of the men emerged from the store to find his panicked partner trying to drive off in the getaway car without him. He shot the driver, who stopped to pick up his partner, but then drove the car into a ditch.

In St. Petersburg, FL, a motorist with a badge, flashing light, and handcuffs pulled over a Cadillac and identified himself as a police officer. The driver turned out to be an off-duty detective, John Buggle, who identified himself and arrested Herbert Ayers, 49, for impersonating a police officer.

In Hollidaysburg, PA, Ivan Sollon Henry, 22, was charged with breaking into the home of the police chief, Edward Plowman, who came home to find him in an upstairs bedroom. "He took a quart of chocolate milk out of the refrigerator and then he went upstairs and started ransacking one of the bedrooms," said Sergeant Dave Shiffler. "He had everything off but his bikini underwear and he was pretending he was asleep in one of the beds."

Authorities caught up with a 61-year-old woman accused of shoplifting hundreds of thousands of dollars in jewelry and eluding police on two continents. She walked into a jewelry store at a Holyoke, MA, shopping mall at the very moment the store manager was reading a flier announcing that she was wanted. According to Holyoke police detective David Beauchemin, the manager looked up and noticed she matched the description given on the flier, then called mall security.

Freedom A. Hunter, 18, tried to cash a $275 check at a bank in Lincoln, NE, but happened to go to a teller whose name and missing driver's license he was using. He was sentenced to six months in jail for forgery.

In Evanston, IL, an 18-year-old man approached a man on a street and offered to sell him a car stereo. The man recognized it as the same stereo that had been stolen from his car the night before and called police.

In McAllen, TX, a former bank president was accused of disguising himself as a masked bandit and attempting to rob the bank he once headed. Before he could get any money, he panicked and fled when a bank employee recognized him.

Police in Norwalk, CT, charged a bank teller with robbing another bank just up the street on his lunch hour. According to Lieutenant Arthur Arway, the teller "punched out, robbed the bank, went home and left the money, and punched back in."

In Coeur d'Alene, ID, Judge James Judd sentenced Jerry Deitz, 33, to three years in prison for perjury. Deitz had been granted a public defender after swearing he was too poor to hire a lawyer and that his only asset was a $600 car. When a prosecutor saw him drive away from the courthouse in a Corvette, however, a check of motor vehicle records revealed that Deitz owned the Corvette, a Triumph sports car, a Ford sedan, a boat, a motorcycle, and two trailers.

At Ruskin High School in Kansas City, MO, a 16-year-old student who was reminded that he owed $30.15 in fines for overdue library books was accused of robbing a jewelry store minutes later and shooting the owner and a customer. Authorities arrested him after he used some of the money to pay his fine.

Police in Tallahassee, FL, arrested 475-pound Wayne Lewis, 24, after finding nearly 11 pounds of crack cocaine hidden in the folds of his stomach. At first the officers found no drugs, but they deepened their search after calling in a police dog, which began sniffing around Lewis's rolls of fat, pointing out the drugs.

Police in St. Petersburg, FL, seeking Kevin Callahan, 32, for questioning in the stabbing of his wife, found him in the hospital after he had been struck by lightning.

James Compton, 34, climbed a water tower in Tracy, CA, and threatened to jump off unless police dropped drug charges against him. After deciding he would rather live, Compton started to come down, but he lost his footing on the ladder and fell 75 feet to his death.

Doctors at the University of Nebraska Medical Center said a 49-year-old AIDS patient apparently had been infected with HIV while beating up gay men. Drs. Paul Carson and Jonathon D. Goldsmith reported in the British medical journal *Lancet* that the man told them he often got small cuts on his hands and large amounts of victims' blood on himself during the beatings. When they told him that he could have brought the disease on himself, Carson said, "He just grunted and shook his head."

In Tanzania, Salimu Hatibu, 27, was convicted of stealing from a church. According to authorities, he fled from the courtroom to avoid a jail sentence and plunged into a river to shake off pursuing police—right into the jaws of a crocodile.

Police in Prestonsburg, KY, arrested Jeannie Jacobs, 18, just hours before her wedding, for shoplifting a $499 wedding gown. When a search of the car that Jacobs was riding in uncovered the gown, a veil, suits, ties, white shoes, apparel for a flower girl, two cushions for ring bearers, a camera, and 10 rolls of film in the trunk, police also arrested Jacobs's sister and a male companion. They did not charge five others in the car, including the groom.

Yorktown, VA, authorities blamed a 33-year-old man for a crime spree that began when he took a woman's car, after telling her he was a mechanic and could fix it. At a service station, he pumped 10 gallons of gas and left without paying. Shortly afterward, he ate a prime rib dinner and drank three bourbon-and-cokes, again leaving without paying. Next, he showed up at another restaurant and ordered a mixed drink and a seafood platter, and left without paying the bill. Finally, he was arrested after reportedly downing two submarine sandwiches and a beer at a Pizza Hut, and leaving without paying. York County sheriff P. S. Williams commented, "He must have been a mighty hungry boy."

A man with a shotgun trying to hold up a bank in Oslo, Norway, encountered fundamentalist preacher Hans Bratterud, a customer in the bank. Bratterud ordered the gunman to stop and shouted for Jesus to help. When the robber turned toward Bratterud, another customer came to his rescue and hit the robber on the head with a large ashtray.

When a man delivered a large plywood crate to a flea market in New Port Richey, FL, just before closing, owner Tom Wellman said he became suspicious and opened the box right away. Inside, he found a man wearing sunglasses and gloves. The man, Robert Raymond Gehm, 37, explained to sheriff's deputies that he had planned to crawl out of the box after everyone left and steal from the flea market.

In Providence, RI, Donna Miller, who was on welfare when she won $14.7 million in a Lotto America drawing, was charged with welfare fraud, food-stamp fraud, medical-assistance fraud, and filing a false document, after she disclosed in an interview with the Providence *Journal* that her employed husband lived with her. She had been collecting benefits on the basis of her claim that he didn't live with her. She pleaded no contest and was ordered to repay $54,000 in benefits she had collected illegally.

In the aftermath of the 1992 Los Angeles riots, police charged Sergio Hernandez, 28, with looting after finding stolen television sets and other electronics gear at his home near the heavily looted south-central neighborhood. Hernandez, who won $3 million in the California lottery in 1989, now receives $120,000 a year.

Two men who stole a tape deck from an electronics store in Annapolis, MD, tried to elude police by turning onto a side street. The street led to the parking lot of police headquarters, where the suspects were nabbed by two detectives leaving the station on their way to the robbery scene. "They couldn't believe what was going on," Officer Dermott Hickey said. "These two people just got dumped in their laps."

Two hours after his car was stolen in White Hall, AR, Samuel Jones was standing in the parking lot where he worked when a man stopped to ask him directions. The man was driving Jones's car. Jones managed to signal to a security guard that he needed help. He was still giving directions when the police arrived and arrested Stanley Turner Norton of Chicago.

Dave Matthews, a journalist for KOAT-TV in Roswell, NM, was monitoring police radio calls when he heard a report of a burglary in progress at his home address. He called home and when his answering machine picked up, he yelled, "Drop that right now, and get the hell out of my house." Matthews then heard another police radio call saying the burglars were fleeing the house. Alerted by a neighbor, police arrested two teenagers.

After watching the movie *Point Break*, about a bank-robbing surfer gang, three boys in Havre de Grace, MD, decided knocking off a bank would be a "neat idea," according to the mother of a 12-year-old gang member. He, his 14-year-old brother, and a 13-year-old schoolmate burst into the First National Bank of North East armed with a loaded .20-gauge sawed-off shotgun and a loaded .22-caliber pistol. Police caught the trio when the cab they had called for their getaway showed up late.

Victims, Bystanders, and Passersby

For every crime, there is a victim. Or some hapless soul who just happens to get in the way. Weirdness has a way of tangling these people in its web as it does the willing participants on both sides of the law. The way these cases turn out, though, sometimes you wonder if there really is such a thing as an innocent bystander.

While Thomas Edmonds's car was legally parked in a two-hour parking zone without meters in the District of Columbia, city workers came by and installed meters on the street. When Edmonds returned to his car before his two hours were up, he found he had been issued a ticket for parking at an expired meter.

Police in Auburn, WA, searching for a knife-wielding suspect, tried to arrest Alvin Euell, 33, but he fled. Officers gave chase and caught him, then took him to the police station, where he stopped breathing. Authorities said that he died because during the chase he had tried to swallow a plastic bag containing marijuana. Witnesses later told police that Euell was not the knife wielder.

In Los Angeles, four people trying to escape a drive-by shooting that had already wounded three of them, ran into a store for protection. According to police lieutenant Mike Downing, they startled the snoozing store owner, who mistook them for robbers and opened fire, shooting the fourth person, a 32-year-old man.

A man in Carol Stream, IL, reported to police that his doorbell rang but when he answered it nobody was there. But someone had placed on his lawn two chairs, two automobile tires, four hubcaps, two endtables, a mattress, and a pumpkin. The man told police that similar incidents had occurred earlier in the year.

Wendy Ellington announced she was suing a Tampa, FL, drugstore whose photo developers copied a set of nude photos of her taken by her boyfriend, who then circulated them at parties. About 150 frantic women called Ellington's lawyer, Matthew Powell, who had come into possession of several albums of similar photos. The callers wanted to know if their nude photos were part of the collection.

In Treviso, Italy, a bandit panicked during a factory payroll holdup and fired as he fled, killing an accomplice he mistook for a pursuing police officer.

In Miami, Nelson Echazabal, 25, caught Claude Cherubin, 22, burglarizing his home. Instead of calling the police, Echazabal suggested they team up to break into someone else's home. Shortly after the heist, police arrested Cherubin for an earlier botched robbery. He told them about Echazabal. The next day, they watched Echazabal try to break into two houses. When he succeeded on the third try, they arrested him.

In Sanford, FL, convicted rapist Mark Edward McCulloch said his life was ruined by Seminole Circuit Court judge Kenneth Leffler. The judge rejected a prison sentence worked out in a plea bargain and called McCulloch's victim a "pitiful woman" and "a victimizer of men." "I was ready to go to jail," McCulloch said, explaining that he had accepted a 4½-year prison term but instead was placed on probation for two years. "I can't walk out of the door without fear of losing my life. He put me at risk. Anyone can take a shot at me."

In Oxnard, CA, a 52-year-old woman called the police twice to complain about rowdy teenagers drinking outside her home and gave the cops her name and address. Four hours after the second call, an officer showed up and arrested her. He explained that when they ran a check of her name, they found a warrant against her for an outstanding traffic ticket from two years earlier. Although she claimed that she had paid the fine, she was arrested and spent several hours in jail before posting bail.

Danny Shaune Clemons, 32, was standing on a train station platform in Greensburg, PA, less than an hour after being released from the State Correctional Institution where he had spent five years for burglary and assault, when two men robbed him of his train fare home.

Å̃

In Omaha, NE, Lavone Stennis and her brother stopped by the house of their brother, James E. Stennis, 48, to visit. When no one answered the door, Lavone Stennis called police and told them James was inside, that he could be suicidal, and that he had a gun. The police department's Emergency Reaction Unit surrounded the house at about 1 p.m., called to Stennis with bullhorns to come out, and repeatedly dialed his telephone for the next six hours. Stennis emerged just before 7 p.m. and explained that he had gotten drunk that morning, returned home about noon, fallen asleep, and hadn't heard the commotion outside.

Authorities in Milwaukee declined to press charges against a 300-pound woman who killed her 160-pound husband during an argument by sitting on him. The woman explained that she had been the victim of abuse.

In Trenton, NJ, Carlos Rodriguez, 22, called his friend Miguel Perez, 18, and told him two masked men were attacking another friend near their homes. Police said Rodriguez and Daniel Barreto, 22, then put on stocking masks and waited, hoping to frighten Perez, and then to pull off their masks and have a good laugh. Their prank backfired when Perez encountered the two masked men in the rainy darkness, pulled his own knife, and stabbed one of them in the chest. The victim was Rodriguez, who pulled off his mask and identified himself to Perez before he died.

When Larry Lands of Potosi, MO, shot a turkey, he put it and his shotgun in the trunk of his car and drove to a neighbor's house. While his 16-year-old son was pulling the turkey out of the trunk, it began thrashing around. Its claw hit the trigger of the loaded shotgun, which fired through the side panel of the car, hitting Lands in the leg. Washington County sheriff Ron Skiles said Lands faced a fine for hunting a week before the start of turkey season.

When her ex-boyfriend beat her up, Petty Officer Francine Adams, 27, suffered a concussion and missed two days of work. Instead of getting help from the Navy, Adams received an official warning to "avoid abusive relationships" or face disciplinary action or discharge. "It's not a blaming of the victim," explained Lieutenant Julie Tinker, a Navy lawyer who was Adams's supervisor at Oceana Naval Air Station in Virginia. "It's getting her to take responsibility for the situation because she was allowing this to happen to her."

John Smith, 46, was recovering from a heart transplant at London's Harefield Hospital when he was mugged. The thief made off with Smith's wallet after binding and gagging him in his hospital bed.

Anthony Wilcox, 65, of Sherman Oaks, CA, was touring Liverpool, England, when muggers dragged him into an alley, broke his nose, and stole his $10,000 Cartier watch. Wilcox told police that a "good Samaritan" passing by helped him to a hospital but stole about $1,200 that he was carrying in a money belt.

Authorities at London's Central Criminal Court said that three men who had been arrested for raping Sandra Harris, 25, were falsely accused. Harris admitted that she was a lesbian who'd had sexual intercourse with a man because she wanted to have a baby, then fabricated the rape story because she could not face her female lover.

Clarence Lewis, 49, was arrested in LaPlace, LA, for killing his wife. Lewis told authorities that her death was an accident, explaining that he had been trying to shoot the television set when he hit Sara Lewis instead.

Oakland, CA, authorities investigating the deaths of Frank Dan Batcheller, 39, and Gwenna Alice Twose, 35, whose bodies were found in Batcheller's bedroom, concluded that Batcheller had committed suicide by discharging a 12-gauge shotgun and that Twose was shot accidentally when she got in the line of fire.

Police in Fort Lauderdale, FL, charged John Williams, 30, with extorting $5,000 from an 84-year-old man. Then Williams sent someone to pick up bail money from the confused victim, got out of jail, and stole from him again.

In England, Richard Weston, 23, of Nottingham, was leaving a police station, where he had reported his car stolen, when he saw it waiting at a traffic light. He ran in front of the vehicle to stop it, but the thieves accelerated, hurling him into the air.

A 20-year-old man and a friend were at a grocery store in Union Gap, WA, when two men approached them and offered to sell them a chain saw. One of the sellers then pulled a gun and forced the two victims into their own car. The robbers drove to a remote area and tried to remove two rings and a watch from the 20-year-old man's left hand. When they couldn't, they fired up the chain saw, cut off the victim's left hand, grabbed the jewelry, and fled.

In Houston, Priscilla Brayboy, 32, who suspected her husband Joe of having an affair, took a friend along to help her find him. They spotted a gray Volvo that Brayboy thought was her husband's in a driveway. Brayboy stopped at the house and knocked on the door. When a woman answered, Brayboy tried to force her way in, only to be shot dead by a man inside the house.

Brayboy's friend began running down the street screaming and noticed another gray Volvo parked in another driveway a few houses away. The woman went to that house and found Joe Brayboy inside.

⚖️

New York City cab driver Inayatullah Malik, 33, was severely burned when a fare doused him with gasoline and set him on fire. While at the New York Hospital-Cornell Medical Center burn unit, he was shocked when nurses wheeled a new patient, who had also suffered severe burns, into his room. Malik identified the newcomer as his attacker.

Minutes before his high school graduation ceremony was to begin in San Francisco, honor student Calvin Wong was arrested and led away in handcuffs. He spent two weeks in a maximum-security prison on charges of kidnapping, first-degree robbery, and unlawful imprisonment before being cleared when his appearance in a police lineup proved that his arrest was a case of mistaken identity. Police said they kept Wong in custody for so long because they had to delay the lineup when they couldn't find enough Asian prisoners to stand in it.

The Wrong Arm of the Law

The good guys don't always wear white. Sometimes they adorn themselves in murky brown. Maybe they started out smart, but hanging around crooks has rubbed off on them. Stupidity may not be hereditary, but it very often is contagious.

Before David Cotto, 20, of Brooklyn, NY, could carry out his threat to stab himself in his family's apartment, a police sergeant sprayed chemical mace in his face, then two officers opened fire. Cotto died when nine of their eleven rounds hit him.

In the Philippines, police had to kill Enrique Quinanola, 21, to prevent him from committing suicide. Quinanola first tried to hang himself at his home in Cebu City, but relatives cut the rope and brought him to a hospital. As doctors prepared to sedate him, Quinanola slipped away and ran to a nearby restaurant, where he grabbed a knife and slashed his wrists. Police tried to subdue Quinanola but, according to witnesses, he put up such a struggle that the officers shot him in the leg and chest. He died moments later.

A police officer in Taft, CA, shot and killed Baxter Purser, 27, in front of his home while other officers and Kern County sheriff's deputies were trying to talk him out of committing suicide.

Police in Naples, FL, wanted to use a sting operation to nab drug sellers in the affluent resort's few black neighborhoods. The 75-member police department had only one black officer, so white detectives wore blackface makeup and "colorful" clothes for the undercover operation, which was dubbed "Operation Al Jolson." They made 33 arrests.

Police officers in Gallup, NM, directing traffic around a mock accident to test emergency preparedness, flagged two cars into a real collision.

The federal government gave Newark, NJ, $101,791 in 1991 to fund a five-year program to fight street crime by installing 24-hour surveillance cameras. In the 1970s, a similar program in Miami Beach, FL, was scrapped after several years because police had a hard time recruiting people to watch the monitors. Sunlight often obscured the images and it wasn't cost effective.

When Thai reporters asked Bangkok's chief of police, Viroj Pao-in, if his officers were taking bribes from brothel owners, he said that was impossible because brothels do not exist in the Thai capital. The next day, Crime Division commander Rangsit Yanothai told reporters, "There are numerous brothels in Bangkok." When told of his chief's remarks, Pao-in quickly withdrew his comment.

District of Columbia parking-enforcement officials twice ticketed a Lincoln Town Car limousine parked on Capitol Hill with its engine running for 15 hours. Authorities said that at one point a traffic attendant tapped on a window to try to awaken the lone occupant, then ticketed the car when he didn't respond. Finally, a passerby noticed the motor running, the key in the ignition, and "a number" of tickets on the windshield. She opened the driver's door to find the man on the floor, dead from a gunshot to the right temple. The city gave the two enforcement aides who ticketed the car a day off, according to Department of Public Works spokeswoman

Schanolia Barnes, "to relieve stress" and to deal with the "morbidity" of the incident.

When a Thurston County, WA, emergency operator answered a call but heard only heavy breathing, Sheriff's Deputy Gary Daurelio was dispatched to investigate. He concluded that the caller was a 150-pound pig he found alone inside the house. Daurelio said the pig escaped from its backyard pen, pushed open the back door of the house, went inside, knocked over the telephone and somehow managed to dial 911.

In Bombay in 1982, nearly 22,000 police constables demanding better pay and working conditions went on an all-day rampage, torching hundreds of cars and smashing shop windows.

In the Philippines, the warden of the jail in Cotabato, Lieutenant Evaristo Ordinaria, took a week's leave to attend a seminar on jail management. When he returned, he found that nine inmates had escaped during his absence.

Relatives of a motorist killed in a car crash in Mishawaka, IN, were surprised when they attended a George Thorogood concert three weeks later and found two strangers sitting in the victim's seats. The pair said they bought the tickets from a relative of Leroy Witucki, who turned out to be the police officer who investigated the fatal accident. Witucki, a 10-year veteran of the force, resigned after admitting that he stole the tickets while examining the victim's body.

⚖

San Ramon, CA, police officer Joe Gorton arrested a fugitive by dressing up as a chicken and pretending he was delivering a singing telegram.

A security guard at a Fort Lauderdale, FL, museum called 911 when he couldn't awaken a woman he found in the lobby. Responding medics identified the victim as a still-life figure by artist Duane Hanson.

⚖

When Ron Carey, 56, who played Officer Levitt on television's "Barney Miller," and New Jersey state senator Carmen Orechio went to lunch at a restaurant in Trenton, Orechio parked his car in a restaurant spot reserved for the handicapped. Several out-of-uniform police, who were taking part in a rally next door outside city hall to protest the suspension of a fellow officer, yelled at the two to move the car. Carey reportedly shouted back no, then got into a heated dispute with the officers, who accused him of yelling "you banana brains" and "I'm from 'Barney Miller,' you idiots," before he got so out of control that they had to summon a police van to cart him off to jail.

Philippine's vice president Joseph Estrada personally arrested two high-ranking police officers suspected of having ties to a kidnap gang that targets Filipino-Chinese businessmen. Estrada, a former film actor who played a vigilante, invited Major Jose Pring and Major Timoteo Zarcal to a news conference at his home, then dramatically produced a surprise witness against them.

Ten police officers and a dispatcher in Sandusky, OH, were charged with stealing the Girl Scout cookies they were supposed to distribute.

A $240,000 Minneapolis gun buy-back program ran out of money in just six days when authorities intending to take handguns off the street offered $50 for any gun, no questions asked. After suspending the program to seek funding from private donors, authorities announced resumption of the buy-back, explaining that now people surrendering pistols would get the $50 but people with rifles and shotguns would have to settle for tickets to Minnesota Twins baseball games.

In Schwerin, Germany, two undercover police officers dressed as skinheads drove by a disco just after fifty real skinheads had raided the building and wrecked it. Authorities said an angry crowd mistook the officers for part of the gang and attacked them. Terrified of being lynched, one of the officers pulled his gun and blasted away, wounding two of the townspeople and his own partner.

While Essex County, NJ, acting prosecutor James Mulvihill was inside a Newark church telling an audience how his office was fighting auto theft, four youngsters stole his unmarked county car parked outside. After returning to where he had parked and finding only the car's lock lying in the gutter, Mulvihill explained that a member of his staff was supposed to be watching the car, but mistakenly thought it was across the street when it was really around the corner. Police recovered the car after a high-speed chase through three towns and arrested the 11-year-old driver and a 14-year-old companion. The other two youngsters fled.

In Omaha, NE, Clarence Stelly, 22, wanted for shooting two convenience store clerks during separate robbery attempts, tried to surrender but found the police station closed. It was Sunday and the front desk was staffed only on week-days, so that more police could be on the street on weekends. Friends had to drive Stelly twenty-five blocks before they found a police officer who would arrest him.

Authorities accused Stelly of being the "Count-down Robber," so named because he told the clerks to open their cash registers on a count of 10. In both cases, the clerks were too slow, provoking the robber to shoot them and flee without taking any money.

Company officials at an Amoco Corp. plant in Wood River, IL, admitted secretly installing a camera in the women's shower room. Amoco spokesperson Howard Miller explained that the camera was being used to check reports of a man sneaking into the room and insisted it only showed people "from the shoulders up."

The Dutch government ruled that prostitutes would have to charge sales tax. Noting "that they are to be treated as entrepreneurs just as any other," Finance Ministry spokeswoman Mariette van Vucht explained that the new tax law lets prostitutes deduct sales tax paid on job-related items, such as condoms and beds.

Bulgaria's customs service reported that to stop smugglers ninety of its officers had been trained in extrasensory perception. Authorities explained that those trained in ESP confiscated more contraband than their colleagues who rely on conventional methods.

When police in Sri Lanka arrested a man after finding a condom in his wallet, the medical director of the Family Planning Association, Sriyani Basnayake, protested to the police that "condoms are not a security threat." But police were skeptical, according to the state-owned newspaper, *Daily News,* which quoted one police officer as saying, "Why would anyone want to carry a condom in his wallet, unless of course he was up to some mischief?"

Lack of money in Poland's prison system forced one institution with overdue bills for food and fuel to cut phone service, remove radios from prisoners' cells, and begin charging inmates a fee for using their own televisions. Chief accountant Cezary Rosinski admitted that the situation had gotten so bad that he was avoiding creditors by hiding in the cells.

Honolulu police in 1983 began recruiting private citizens to have sex with prostitutes and then testify against them. The program came to light during a pretrial hearing for a woman charged with prostitution. The 26-year-old night manager of a Waikiki hotel testified that police gave him money and told him to drive around until he picked up a prostitute. He said he complied out of a sense of "civic duty." He said he then paid the defendant $70 for sex, whereupon she was arrested.

Police in Des Moines, WA, hired Robert Berdue, 29, a convicted rapist, to have sex with suspected prostitutes. Despite Berdue's conviction, Police Chief Martin Pratt said that the department paid him to engage in sexual acts as an informant in a 1992 sting operation aimed at protecting the public from organized prostitution.

When Kelso, WA, police officers Ernie Moore and Darrell Stair told a 42-year-old assault suspect holed up in his attic to come down or they would send up a dog, Stair convinced the man that they had a dog by barking and growling like one. The suspect immediately surrendered.

Japanese plastic surgeon Mitsuo Yoshimura approached police, offering his services to *yakuza* gangsters who renounce crime. According to the *Mainichi Shimbun* newspaper, the surgeon replaces gangsters' ritually severed finger, the mark of membership in the crime syndicate, with their little toe.

The procedure proved so popular with ex-gangsters that Yoshimura reported he was booked up six months ahead, despite the fact that patients have to pay the $6,000 for the procedure themselves. Japan's national health insurance pays for reattachment of any severed finger except the little finger—an exclusion specifically designed to keep the *yakuza* from using up the insurance fund.

The California Court of Appeal ruled in 1985 that a prison guard should not have been fired even though he was caught off-duty running through an empty elementary schoolyard wearing women's underwear.

In Stuart, FL, a woman complained to police some thirty times that a man had been peering in her window and masturbating almost daily for five years. But each time she complained, police explained that they could not spare any officers for surveillance. Finally, she bought a video camera, set it up in the bushes outside her window, and caught the man in the act.

While cameras from the television show "Cops" recorded a late-night raid of the home of a suspected crack dealer, police in King County, WA, kicked in the door, charged upstairs with their guns drawn, and ordered the man, woman, and four children out of their beds and onto the floor. When they found no drugs, the officers realized they had hit the wrong side of a duplex. "They pulled me out of bed and put a gun on me," the woman said. "Here I am with my butt showing, and I see the camera."

Burrillville, RI, police sergeant Walter J. Korzeniowski, 46, who had been on sick leave for two years, collecting $461 a week plus benefits, was ordered back to work after he won the title of Mr. America at a bodybuilding contest.

In Omaha, NE, the emergency room at Clarkson Hospital was left unattended for about an hour after the only doctor on duty, Bruce Harvey, was arrested because he was slow to respond to a police request to draw blood from a drunken-driving suspect.

In Dalton, GA, police ordered the Harvest Ministries shelter for the homeless to close because it didn't have a parking lot. Sheila Reed, the shelter's director, objected, pointing out that the homeless don't drive cars.

After accidentally opening fire inside the police station and shooting holes in his office walls, David Milchan, police chief of Pinellas Park, FL, punished himself with a suspension.

Police in Sydney Mines, Nova Scotia, raided their own Christmas party for not having a liquor license.

In Oregon City, OR, sheriff's deputy Todd R. Rollins, 24, was dreaming that someone attacked him when he apparently grabbed his 9mm semiautomatic pistol from his bedside. He awakened to find he had shot himself. Rollins said that his wife slept through the episode and had to be awakened to drive him to the hospital.

Captive Audiences

Iron bars do not a prison make, but throw in some surly guards and a general lack of amenities, and you've got a pretty dismal situation. Plus, if criminals are already stupid, then criminals who've been caught and sentenced to jail are the low end of the totem pole—about the intellectual equal of gerbils in a cage. And just as desperate to get out.

Three convicted murderers at West Virginia Penitentiary in Moundsville escaped after taking four months to dig a 16-foot deep, 32-foot long tunnel from the prison greenhouse to the other side of the prison wall. Authorities found the tunnel equipped with electric lighting, fans for ventilation, and even a radio. Police immediately arrested one of the men, Fred D. Hamilton, 34, after he abducted a motorist and forced him to drive 150 miles to Erie, PA. The driver said Hamilton told him they got rid of the dirt from the tunnel by putting it in bags, then telling the guards that it was peat moss and rich topsoil and getting them to haul it home for their gardens.

An appeals court in St. Louis denied a request by Steven Goodwin, 34, an inmate at the federal prison in Springfield, MO, that prison officials provide a container for his semen, which would be rushed to his 30-year-old wife so that she could have his baby. The three-judge panel said that granting Goodwin's request would be too burdensome and costly. What's more, Judge Frank J. Magill said, "If the [Bureau of Prisons] were forced to allow male prisoners to procreate, whatever the means, it would have to confer a corresponding benefit to its female prisoners."

Fourteen death-row inmates in California filed a lawsuit in U.S. District Court asking the state to allow them to father children through conjugal visits or artificial insemination. One of the inmates named in the suit, Herbert J. Coddington, had been sentenced to death for killing his two children in a custody dispute with his wife.

According to the inmates' attorney, Carter R. King, the suit contended that laws banning prisoners from procreating constituted cruel and unusual punishment. Acknowledging that the Supreme Court had denied past requests for conjugal visits for condemned inmates, citing security, King noted, "Obviously, artificial insemination doesn't create a security risk."

Nine former inmates of the Tallahatchie County Jail in Mississippi filed a lawsuit, claiming the $10 daily fee they were charged for their stay violated their rights to due process and equal protection of the law. The county charges the fee to all who spend time in jail, regardless of the length of stay or the outcome of the trial. In fact, inmates are not released until they pay it.

One plaintiff said he was stuck in jail for 90 days trying to raise $2,500 for bail. Even after he made bail, he remained in jail because he could not come up with the $900 rent he owed on the cell. He was released three months later only after reaching a settlement with the sheriff.

Taiwan's Justice Ministry proposed that condemned prisoners who agree to donate organs after death be rewarded by being shot in the head instead of the customary execution method of being placed face down in a sandpit and shot through the heart.

Jesus Cruz, 38, an inmate at the Bronx House of Detention in New York, was assigned to watch prisoners who might commit suicide. Two months later, Cruz was found hanged from a shower with a piece of cloth. His death was ruled a suicide.

Investigating a series of threatening phone calls that terrified some residents of a St. Louis suburb, authorities traced the calls to a pay phone used by inmates in the Essex County Jail in Newark, NJ. The investigators said they do not know why the calls were made or why the 27 Chesterfield, MO residents who complained accepted the collect calls, which told them family members had been kidnapped or ordered them to perform sexual acts. Some victims hung up immediately, but others stayed on the line as long as twenty minutes.

At a minimum-security state prison in Shirley, MA, Gordon Benjamin III was granted parole, but decided to remain in prison another two months to appear as Sir Lancelot in an inmate production of *Camelot*. Because prisoners had been transferred, the cast had already lost four King Arthurs, two Merlins, and one Squire Dap before the production opened.

William Sibila used the old bedsheet-rope trick to try to escape from the prison ward of New York's Nassau County Medical Center. The distance to the ground was 55 feet, but Sibila misjudged and made the rope only 20 feet long. He was killed when he fell the remaining 35 feet onto a cement landing.

At Boston's Deer Island jail, a prisoner who climbed onto the jail roof had only one demand for officials trying to coax him down: Name all six children on *The Brady Bunch*. Deputy Penal Commissioner George Romanos says even though nobody could come up with the right answer (Marcia, Greg, Jan, Peter, Cindy, Bobby), the inmate got tired of waiting after five hours and came down anyway.

Joseph Jenkins was sent to prison in New Orleans to serve a 16-month sentence for stealing shirts from a department store. After only two days in jail, deputies ordered the 51-year-old vagrant to leave his cell despite his protests. A week later, he returned to the prison and demanded his cell back. At first, deputies refused to take him. Jenkins wouldn't leave this time, and after a few hours the deputies put him behind bars. Judge Jerome Winsberg, who originally sentenced Jenkins, said the sheriff's office told him that Jenkins's release was a mistake.

Authorities in Pulaski, TN, feared that Pat and Pete Bondurant, 300-pound identical twin brothers charged with killing the same woman, might team up to overpower guards and escape. So they ordered the pair placed in separate jails.

In Chicago, a man convicted of theft and sentenced to stay home wearing an electronic anklet, ordered a pizza and robbed the delivery person. The next day he lured an eighteen-year-old man to the house on the pretext of a drug deal, then killed him in the doorway. "The program did what it was intended to do," an official pointed out, "keep the man at home."

When millionaire James Sullivan, 50, pleaded no contest to lying under oath when questioned about a traffic ticket he had received for driving his red Rolls Royce with an expired tag and driver's license, he was sentenced to a year's house arrest. Jail officials assigned to keep track of him had to further restrict him to the first floor of his two-story, $4.9 million mansion in Palm Beach, FL, when they discovered that their monitoring equipment couldn't cover all 17,000 square feet.

A check for $26,477 from the city of Tracy, CA, to San Joaquin County treasurer–tax collector Thomas Russell was mistakenly sent to a prisoner in the county jail with the same name. The other Thomas Russell, 22, who had been arrested on a burglary charge, used $6,500 of the windfall to post bail, then left town with the remaining $20,000.

Going to jail in Raymondville, Texas, became a soft sentence once inmates discovered that by lying on their back on the top bunk of their cell and pressing their feet against the ceiling, they could raise the covering and crawl into a space between the ceiling and the roof. They then could use the crawl space to enter the evidence room and steal marijuana or kick a hole in the roof and escape, as at least a dozen did before authorities found out about the crawl space five months later.

"I saw guys actually smile when sentenced to jail," said County Judge Eustolio Gonzales. "They figured it wasn't such a bad deal, when they could get free drugs or leave whenever they wanted."

Two inmates at the Peter Pitchess Honor Rancho in Santa Clarita, CA, got into an argument over whose turn it was to use the telephone. The dispute escalated into a brawl, which spread to other inmates, injuring twenty-five.

At a Los Angeles County prison camp, two inmates negotiating the sale of a bag of potato chips began arguing, then fighting. About forty of the prison's ninety-two inmates joined in before twenty-four deputies in riot gear restored order.

☙⚖❧

Michael Wayne Carroll, 36, an inmate at the Maryland House of Correction, pleaded guilty to stealing more than $10,000 while he was behind bars. Using forged documents he made on the prison's photocopier, Carroll convinced the state comptroller's office that he was the person entitled to an unpaid $9,771 state tax refund. He also admitted getting $786 from an insurance company after submitting phony bills that showed his car had been damaged. In addition, he was charged with falsifying a claim for the return of a $600 membership in a health club that never opened and trying to get a government-ordered refund from a Pennsylvania campground.

Convicted forger Jean Paul Barrett, 26, escaped from the Pima County, AZ, jail by having a forged release order faxed to jailers.

☙⚖❧

Kavin Peeples was serving 7 to 25 years at Ohio's Orient Correctional Institution for trying to strangle his girlfriend, after having failed to kill himself by drinking insecticide when she broke up with him. Peeples, 29, strangled a fellow prisoner following two more botched suicide tries.

He explained that after failing to die from drinking ink and being unable to work up the courage to hang himself with a bedsheet rope, he figured the only way to succeed at suicide was to kill another inmate. State patrol trooper Richard S. Slater testified that Peeples told him: "I figured if I get arrested for murder, I will get the electric chair and that will be like suicide."

Twenty-five convicted murderers serving life sentences at Philadelphia's Graterford Prison sold 1,900 boxes of Girl Scout cookies to fellow inmates, raising $4,615 for the Girl Scouts. One of the lifers, Gary Kretchmar, accounted for nine hundred of the boxes sold.

⚖

Jessie Lee Baker, 27, who was being held at Atlanta's Fulton County Jail on charges of attempted rape and robbery, was watching the television show "America's Most Wanted" with other inmates when his photograph appeared on the screen as a fugitive in a Florida murder case. Inmates who recognized him chased him back to his cell and summoned jail officials.

Pedro Diaz Ramirez, 26, was leaving jail in St. Paul, MN, after serving a sentence for petty theft when he climbed into an empty police van idling nearby and drove off. Police shot out two rear tires, then chased him for several miles before another officer managed to shoot out a front tire and box the van in.

Acting on a tip, jail officials in Morehead, KY, discovered that the man serving a 30-day sentence was not the person who had been convicted. The authorities ordered the actual guilty person, James Logan, to serve his full sentence. Then they demanded that Clyde James, who had served 16 days of Logan's term, apparently for money, pay the county $320 for lodging.

An escape from a jail in Fairfield, CA, went unnoticed for five hours because no one was watching the security monitoring cameras. Then there was a 55-minute delay in notifying dispatchers, and someone used a wrong computer code that kept the California Highway Patrol from finding out about the break for twelve hours. Solano County sheriff Al Cardoza also told the board of supervisors afterward that a dispatcher, mistaking the escaping inmates for juvenile pranksters, had urged one of the inmates, who fell while scaling a fence, to "try again."

Furrier Daniel Antonovich brought fur coats to show inmates at Riker's Island Correctional Facility and selected some of the women in the New

York prison to model the furs, which cost up to $40,000. "The majority of my customers are black and Hispanic. The churches and jails are full of those," Antonovich explained. "I hope that inmates, after seeing the chic outfits, will be motivated to work hard enough after their release and earn enough money to buy one of the products."

Massachusetts opened the Norfolk County Correctional Center between the north and south lanes of heavily traveled Route 128 in suburban Boston. Besides being the first U.S. jail built in the median of a major highway, it was the first in the state to ban smoking because windows sealed to keep highway car exhaust out trap cigarette smoke inside.

Within days of the opening of the $45-million escape-proof Oklahoma County Jail, four inmates broke out when they discovered that the thick glass blocks in their windows could easily be removed by chipping away the mortar between them. Sheriff J.D. Sharp explained that reinforcements were not put into the windows to save money, but he added, "There's no place that's completely escape-proof."

Florida State Prison authorities conducting a strip search of inmate Mark DeFriest discovered a homemade key that could open doors throughout the facility. An investigation turned up a number of DeFriest's secret hiding places, where guards found several dozen weapons. A further search revealed a plastic bag in DeFriest's rectum that contained 6 homemade handcuff keys, 7 hacksaw blades, 34 razor blades, and $2,000 in cash.

In New Orleans, a six-year prison term for running various scams didn't stop Joseph West, 31. He used the prison computer at the city's Jackson Barracks to collect money from local businesses. Prison officials explained that West used the telephone book to pick firms that he figured had large parking lots, then sent them invoices for painting stripes on their lots. Even though he never painted a stripe, he received at least $8,000 before he was caught when he threatened to use a lawyer to collect one of the bogus bills. Warden Frank Jobert, Jr., observed, "It looks like he went a step too far."

The Renz Correctional Center in Jefferson City, MO, announced it was restricting female inmates to one roll of toilet paper a week after discovering that many of the women were using toilet paper to stuff homemade dolls and clean windows. The local chapter of the National Organization for Women immediately donated three hundred sixty rolls for the inmates.

Texas prison officials were thwarted in their effort to execute murderer Billy Wayne White, 34, by lethal injection because longtime heroin use had scarred his arm so badly that they couldn't locate a vein for the needle. Andy Collins, director of Texas prisons, reported that the execution proceeded after White, whom he called "very cooperative," helped them find a suitable vein.

Arizona ordered that prisoners being executed must strip to their underwear before entering the gas chamber. When family members of some death-row inmates decried the policy as unnecessary humiliation, Mike Arra, spokesperson for the Department of Corrections, explained that it was a safety precaution because the cyanide gas used could collect in clothing, creating a hazard for the prison crew that removes the body.

Needing a job after nine years in federal prison for drug smuggling, Bruce Perlowin, 41, put together a resume, titled "Ex-Marijuana Kingpin Needs a Job." The resume touted his "knack for organization." Perlowin, who was paroled in 1992, ran a fleet of boats and ships that hauled 250 tons of marijuana into California between 1974 and 1983. His sales exceeded $500 million. He said that the 30 resumes he sent out brought 10 positive responses, including an offer for a job as a national sales manager for an "environmentally conscious" company handling a food product harvested in a rain forest.

In Dallas, convicted murderer Robert Hernandez didn't think his 65-year prison sentence for murder was fair. He appealed and won a new trial. The new jury sentenced him to 90 years and added a $10,000 fine.

Five years after Richard Dickinson of Hobart, Australia, stomped his mother to death while listening to Bob Dylan's song, "One More Cup of Coffee for the Road," then sprinkled instant coffee over her body, authorities released him from the psychiatric facility for one night in 1992 to attend a Dylan concert. Dickinson, 25, who admitted killing his 59-year-old mother when she complained because he was playing Bob Dylan's *Desire* album at 4 a.m., was found not guilty by reason of insanity. Doctors decided going to the concert would do him good.

In Texas, three inmates at the Hays County Jail admitted buying hundreds of yards of dental floss at the jail store and braiding it into a ladder, which they said they intended to use to escape. "It was ingenious," U.S. Attorney Gerald Carruth said. "They made the rope out of dental floss and used cardboard salt and pepper containers for stirrups on the ladder."

⚖️

Texas Prison System officials banned the January 1991 issue of *Texas Monthly* from inmate subscribers because they said it contained contraband: a roadmap of the state. The official denial notice said the map, which the magazine had inserted to encourage its readers to travel, "could be used to facilitate an escape."

Lance Todd, an inmate at the Elmwood Correctional Facility in Malpitas, CA, managed to escape through a storm drain. Instead of rushing to freedom, he headed for the nearest Taco Bell. He bought fourteen burritos, then tried to break back into the jail to enjoy the food in his cell. Todd was apprehended when a startled corrections officer looked down and noticed him, Taco Bell bags in hand, looking up at him from under the grate in the storm drain.

⚖️

Officials in San Diego County, CA, discovered that seven years earlier the board of supervisors, to save money, had ordered that the walls of a new jail be built with drywall and styrofoam instead of concrete. Eleven jailbreaks had occurred during those seven years, most from inmates simply punching through walls.

An attempted jailbreak in Okanogan, WA, was foiled when the two inmates trying to escape during the night made so much noise chipping through an eight-inch concrete wall that other prisoners trying to sleep complained to guards, who caught the men in a crawl space. Sheriff Jim Weed said that even if the men had been able to chip through the outside wall, when they broke through they would have found themselves 80 feet above the ground.

In Morgantown, WV, Robert Lee Friend, serving a six-month jail sentence for faking a suicide jump from a bridge, hanged himself in his cell.

During an escape attempt several years earlier, Fred Silva, 48, serving a 40-year sentence in Missouri's Jefferson City Correctional Center, lost his legs from the knees down when he was severely frostbitten. When he finally was fitted with a new pair of artificial legs, he immediately overpowered a guard, commandeered the officer's car, and tried to break out of the prison. Another car blocked his escape.

At Florida's Kissimmee Correctional Center, guards who found a hole cut in the chain-link fence said it was the work of three men who broke into the minimum security prison and tried to steal two 25-inch television sets from the inmates' common room before they were interrupted and fled. Police said the men also entered several dormitories at the prison. When inmates challenged them, they pretended to be guards.

Disorder in the Court

*From the standpoint of antics, courtrooms are the
sideshow of the criminal justice system. You always thought Perry Mason was clever for getting
guilty people to confess, but given the nature of
guilty people, sooner or later they'll trip themselves
up—if they don't just blurt out their guilt inadvertently. Courtrooms bring crooks, cops, judges, and
lawyers together in one grand carnival.*

A Superior Court judge in Rhode Island refused
to grant a mistrial to a defendant who beat up
his lawyer in front of the jury. "You sell me out,
and I will kill you," shouted Steven G. Rollins,
who had 64 convictions, including one for murder, as he leapt on his lawyer after being led
into court for closing arguments.

The attorney, Robert Testa, who suffered a
mild concussion, asked to withdraw from the
case because he was considering pressing
charges against his client. Judge Americo Campanella denied Testa's request.

Rollins then apologized to the judge, explaining that he didn't think Testa was representing him adequately. Campanella forgave

him but refused to grant a mistrial after prosecutor Carl Levin suggested that Rollins had staged the assault to get a new trial. The old trial resumed, and the jury acquitted Rollins.

On trial for a long list of charges stemming from having thrown a Molotov cocktail through the window of an apartment occupied by his girlfriend and her 10-year-old son, Tyrone D. Robinson of Washington, DC, interrupted the second day of proceedings by shrieking, "I'm on fire." Then he pulled a wad of used toilet paper from his pocket and smeared it on his face. The judge declared a mistrial and ordered Robinson held for observation.

He spent the next six months at a mental hospital rocking, moaning, shuddering, and speaking in a language nobody could understand. He also set fire to his bed, barricaded himself in a dormitory and growled and shouted gibberish at the staff, splashed himself with water from the toilet, exposed himself and, the hospital staff reported, on a day he was due in court hadn't had a bowel movement in several days while eating "everything in sight" as if "saving up ammunition."

The judge ordered a new trial, and the day before it was to start Robinson sent word he wanted to meet with the prosecutor. Assistant U.S. Attorney Michael Brittin would agree to the meeting only if Robinson wore handcuffs, waist chains, and leg irons. Duly shackled, Robinson made his first coherent statement in six months, telling Brittin, "I thought I could beat this thing, but it's clear to me that you're not going to let me go." He pleaded guilty to five offenses.

Hakic Ceku, a Yugoslav man charged with possessing firearms and belonging to an armed gang, appeared in court in Malaga, Spain, with his lips sewn shut to avoid making a statement. Ceku then attacked his lawyer with a glass ashtray, prompting a three-day adjournment.

In Pontiac, MI, Christopher Plovie was fighting a drug charge by claiming he had been searched improperly. After his attorney insisted that Oakland County Circuit Court judge Barry Howard inspect the denim jacket Plovie was wearing to show how the search was conducted, Howard did—and found a packet of cocaine. "The judge began laughing so hard he had to take a five-minute break," said assistant prosecutor Brian Zubel. "The defense attorney thought it was amusing. Even the defendant smiled."

In Houston, State District Judge Carl Walker, Jr. denied a defense motion that the jury pool of 50 include at least some people who are no taller than 5 feet to decide the fate of 4-foot-1-inch accused murderer Jeffrey Leibengood. Lawyer John Carrigan explained that his client had faced discrimination all his life because of his height and "he feels that a jury of all tall people would be prejudicial against him." After Walker's ruling, the 5-foot-plus jurors who were chosen found Leibengood guilty. He was sentenced to 50 years.

In Santa Ana, CA, Harry Veltman III, acting as his own lawyer against charges that he sent Olympic gold medal figure skater Katarina Witt some 60 threatening letters and nude photos of himself, asked that his jury be made up only of nymphomaniacs and atheists.

Gayle Fuchs of Sikeston, MO, was found guilty of embezzling more than $168,000 from the bank where she worked. Although federal guidelines prescribe 18 months in prison as the minimum sentence for this crime, Fuchs received only four months after her attorney argued that she was psychologically diminished while embezzling the money because she was distraught over her inability to conceive a child.

Dr. Michael Gilbert, 75, who spent three decades as a court witness testifying about defendants' mental condition, was accused of trying to bribe a police officer to help him find a professional killer who would slay the father of a child who Gilbert believed was being abused. Gilbert announced he would defend himself by claiming insanity, saying he had three experts ready to testify that years of working around the criminally insane had left Gilbert insane himself.

In Roanoke, VA, General District Court, Judge Edward Kidd dismissed indecent exposure charges against a defendant despite testimony by a woman that he flashed her during a heated argument. The man explained that he could not have exposed himself since he had nothing to expose, a condition confirmed by an impromptu medical exam. Prosecutor Joel Branscom conceded, "I think it was one of the better defenses to an indecent exposure charge that I've ever seen."

Pleading guilty to defacing London's subway trains with graffiti, Andrew Hayes, 26, explained to the court that his underground art career was over anyway, because he had developed an allergy to spray paint.

A Denver District Court jury convicted Manuel Bustos Silva, 42, of murdering his common-law wife, Maria Rodriguez, despite his explanation. He claimed that she hexed him by putting pubic hairs in his food, which caused him to go crazy and strangle her.

M. K. O. Abiola, chief of the Yoruba tribe in Nigeria, denied in a Manhattan court that he had 79 children and 26 wives. He was charged by Gloria Uboh-Abiola, who claimed to be one of the wives, when she filed suit for divorce from the reputed billionaire. The correct figure, he explained, was 69 children, four wives, and 18 concubines, one of whom was Uboh-Abiola. The distinction didn't matter to the judge, who dismissed the divorce action on grounds that New York doesn't recognize polygamous marriage.

During his rape trial in Saline County, AR, Circuit Court, Kenneth Morgan, 63, exposed himself to a witness and the jury, then argued that his action was grounds for a mistrial. The motion was denied, and he was convicted.

Witnesses told a court in Liverpool, England, that a man who conned people in bars to buy him drinks by telling a tear-jerking tale that he was suffering from terminal cancer, died when his story convinced one man to take him home and end his suffering by suffocating him with a pillow.

After Bobby LaTulip, 37, was convicted of stealing 18 pallets from a supermarket in Lakeland, FL, his lawyer requested a new trial because a juror hearing the case had a squirrel in her pocket throughout the trial and deliberations. The judge denied the request, saying the squirrel was not enough of a distraction to affect the jurors' deliberations.

Richard and Michelle Kommit of Brookline, MA, used their MasterCard to get a $5,500 cash advance from an automatic teller machine at an Atlantic City, NJ, casino, then refused to pay the bill. The Massachusetts Court of Appeals agreed with their argument that the debt could not be collected because the laws of Massachusetts and Connecticut, where the credit card–issuing bank is located, declare that "a contract to pay money knowingly lent for gambling is void." Their attorney, Neal Brown, argued that the bank had to know the money would be used for gambling because the ATM was right in the "pit," or gambling area of a casino.

In West Palm Beach, FL, one of the prosecution witnesses against Rodney Thomas was the police dog whom Thomas was charged with trying to strangle when police tried to arrest him for burglary. Circuit Court judge Peter Blanc let the dog take the witness stand to show the jury how loud it barked to warn Thomas to surrender.

At his trial for shooting seven people to death at a Sunnyvale, CA, defense contractor firm in 1988, Richard Wade Farley refuted prosecution claims that he planned the attack. Farley testified that it was just a "coincidence" that he bought a semiautomatic shotgun and $1,400 worth of ammunition the week before the shootings. He said he needed them for protection and to impress his ex-girlfriend.

Authorities investigating why Hartford, CT, residents had been excluded from federal grand juries for three years discovered that a computer had listed everybody in the city as dead. Officials explained that the city's name was listed in the wrong place on computer records, forcing the "d" at the end of "Hartford" into the column used for information about jurors. Whenever a resident's name popped up, the computer noted the "d," which stands for death, and a juror questionnaire was not sent.

Willie Williams, 52, was on trial in New Orleans for robbing a convenience store and assaulting the clerk, when prosecutor Sonceree Smith placed a police sketch drawn from the victim's memory next to Williams's face and told the jury to take a long, hard look. Defense attorney Harry

Tervalon looked, too, and he saw a big difference. The man in the sketch had eyebrows. "His entire adult life, Willie Williams has not had eyebrows," Tervalon pointed out to the jury, which acquitted Williams.

⚖

In Hackensack, NJ, a plea bargain was to give murderer Frank Pennington a 30-year-to-life sentence instead of death. As he entered the courtroom for sentencing, he yelled at news photographers: "Don't you have enough (expletive) pictures already? Get the (expletive) out of here! I'm tired of this (expletive)."

When Superior Court judge Charles DiGisi told him the photographers had permission to be there, Pennington replied: "Yeah, well, (expletive) you and this courtroom." Prosecutor Sharon Peiffer immediately withdrew the plea bargain.

To enable 900-pound pawnbroker Sylvanus "Hambone" Smith III to testify against a burglary suspect who police said pawned stolen items with Smith, authorities in Tift County, GA, considered various ways to bring the rarely mobile Smith to the courtroom. These included putting a platform on a forklift and lifting him up to the open windows of a second-floor courtroom, or videotaping Smith's testimony at his home. Because both options posed legal or liability problems, District Attorney David Perry had a bench built in the back of a prison truck with the intention of picking Smith up at his home and backing the truck up to the doors of the courthouse lobby, where chairs would be set up for the jury. Before the trial began and Smith could testify, however, the burglar pleaded guilty.

In San Francisco, after John Daniel Tarpening III, 44, was arrested for selling drugs to an undercover police officer, Judge J. Dominique Olcomendy offered to let Tarpening off with just probation if he would plead guilty to drug dealing. Tarpening declined the plea bargain, demanding instead to be sentenced to the maximum six-year term. He explained that he needed the time to complete his book on space migration.

John Long, 59, of Winamac, IN, a juror in a murder trial, suffered a heart attack just before closing arguments in the trial. He was taken to the hospital, but refused treatment and lied about his symptoms so he could return to the courthouse for the verdict. "I said it was indigestion," Long said. "I had pains in my jaw and across the shoulders. That's almost a dead giveaway, but I had to take that chance." Less than an hour after handing down the guilty verdict, Long collapsed and was taken back to the hospital's intensive care unit.

During a murder trial in Pontiac, MI, court personnel overheard an unidentified juror in the deliberation room shouting to the other jurors that a clairvoyant experience had convinced her the man on trial was not guilty. Shortly afterward, the jurors reported they were deadlocked, but Judge John O'Brien ordered them to resume deliberations.

This Litigious Society

Ridiculous lawsuits are the American way. People have come a long way from the old days of just crying whiplash. Now, everyone sees litigation as their way to get a piece of the pie. Besides, lawyers need the fees; they can't all run for Congress.

Roger Webb, 30, sentenced to 3½ years at the Tokyo Detention House for robbing a convenience store, filed suit against the Japanese government, seeking $3,800 compensation for suffering caused by his imprisonment. Complaining that his 6-by-9-foot cell was too small, the 6-foot-4, 215-pound British citizen said the lack of space was ruining his health and causing intense claustrophobia.

A man who robbed and raped a woman in Great Falls, MT, then stole her car, crashed into another car while trying to make his getaway. The owners of the second car announced that they would try to recover their damages by suing the rape victim.

Three years after Tawana Hammond, the first female to play high school football in Carroll County, MD, was seriously injured during her first scrimmage game, she filed a $1.5 million lawsuit against the county school board. Hammond, who was a 5-foot-10, 150-pound junior playing fullback and safety in August 1989 when she ruptured her pancreas and had to be hospitalized for four months, charged that school officials failed to warn her adequately that playing football was dangerous.

Convicted bank robber Mark Chirico of Amsterdam, NY, announced that he was suing the FBI for libel. He explained that after the agency arrested him for robbing a bank in El Cajon, CA, it noted that he resembled the "Clearasil Bandit"—named for his acne-scarred skin—who was wanted in eight other area bank robberies. "They [the FBI] have this fondness for putting these nicknames on people," Chirico said. "I don't know how the 'B.O. Bandit' feels, but I feel pretty lousy."

After New York robbery suspect Gregory Pierre's oversized ears helped victims pick him out at police lineups, the National Foundation for Facial Reconstruction offered him free reconstructive surgery. It explained that an anonymous donor said Pierre's ears may have psychologically scarred him.

Eleven women filed suit against Elvis Presley impersonator Michael (Little Elvis) Myers of Carson, CA, charging that he bilked them of as much as $100,000. They claimed that while dating them, he charged items on their credit cards and ran up their telephone bills.

In Santa Ana, CA, Joseph de Nobili, 76, filed a breach of contract lawsuit against a mortuary that let his mother's frozen body thaw before he could find a way to preserve it. Lena de Nobili died in 1975 at age 92. Her son, a doctor, spent the next 15 years developing a liquid solution to prevent bacteria growth that causes bodies to decay so he could preserve her in a stainless steel coffin with a hydraulically operated lid that he could open to view her.

In the meantime, he kept her body refrigerated at Harbor Lawn-Mount Olive Mortuary. In 1990, while de Nobili was having surgery in Italy, Harbor Lawn workers unplugged the refrigerator containing his mother and shipped the unrefrigerated body to San Diego for burial, explaining that de Nobili hadn't paid the $500 monthly storage fee since 1984. He retrieved her body, which was undamaged because he had already begun bathing it with his solution.

Three bystanders wounded in a 1988 shootout between rival Japanese gangs in Hiroshima sued one of the gangs. The *yakuza*, Japan's equivalent of the mafia, avoided a trial by agreeing to pay the victims about $70,000. The gang also agreed to pay about $10,500 to the railroad, which had claimed the shootout delayed trains and damaged the station.

Vicki Long filed a lawsuit in Atlanta demanding child support from the Rev. Donal Keohane, a Roman Catholic priest whom she accused of fathering her daughter. When blood tests proved conclusively that Keohane could not have been the father, Long contended that Keohane should be ordered to pay anyway. Keohane conceded that he once agreed to provide $350 a month to support the child, but only as a desperate promise to keep Long from publicizing her charge.

Having too many wives proved embarrassing to Sir Wiwa Korowi, the new governor-general of Papua New Guinea. When he chose Nancy, the younger of his two wives, to accompany him to London to be sworn in by Queen Elizabeth, his senior wife, Sonya, complained about being snubbed and accused the country's "Big Man" of making himself small by not acknowledging all his wives and children when taking office. She demanded a divorce.

While negotiations for a settlement were under way, a former wife previously unknown to the public, Ellepe Nomi, who divorced Sir Wiwa in 1985, entered the fray seeking revenge against Sonya. "We were happily married until she came in," Nomi charged. "She is not his first wife. If she didn't stick her nose into our marriage, we would not have separated."

In Denver, the widow of a USAir pilot, who claimed her husband's fatal brain hemorrhage was an accident caused by having sex with another woman, lost her suit against his insurance company seeking accidental death benefits. U.S. District Court judge John Kane ruled that sex is "not an accident as contemplated in the law."

Detroit resident James Blakely filed suit against the *Detroit Free Press* and the *Detroit News*, demanding the newspapers drop their syndicated horoscopes and pay him $9 million for the suffering that astrology caused him. Noting that horoscopes destroyed his marriage and have caused "an enormous amount of problems" in his life, the 19-page handwritten lawsuit contended that horoscopes are a consumer fraud and the devil's work because they predict events that will not occur.

David Hampton, 27, filed a $100 million lawsuit against playwright John Guare for turning his scam into a Tony-nominated Broadway play. *Six Degrees of Separation* is about a man pretending to be actor Sidney Poitier's son who gets white liberal parents to take him in and give him money by claiming to be a friend of their children. Hampton, who was convicted of the same thing, said he had the idea first. New York State Supreme Court justice Edward Lehner dismissed the suit, explaining that Hampton's criminal schemes were not protected by copyright law.

After she was involved in a traffic accident, Donna Vallah of Nashville, TN, thought at first she had suffered no injuries, but said that within a month after the accident her left breast implant started to deflate. By the time she had surgery a month later, the right implant had also deflated. Vallah sued the other driver, and the jury awarded her $11,500 to cover the cost of replacing both implants.

A week later, a Philadelphia jury awarded Philomena Abruzzese, 62, $10 million because her plastic surgeons had gone too far while reducing her breasts.

Michael G. Vaughn, 44, of Lexington, KY, filed a lawsuit against the Shriners, claiming that the secret initiation rite humiliated and hurt him. He said that at one point during the ceremony, he was blindfolded and told to lie on a table and pull down his boxer shorts. Then his bare buttocks were given a jolt of electricity with a stick wired to a 12-volt motorcycle battery. Attorneys defending the Oleika Shrine Temple said they would bring in witnesses who would testify that the ritual was not painful, but fun.

Convicted murderer Walter J. Wood filed suit against the Utah State Prison, claiming that the prison caused him trauma by allowing him to escape with two other convicts. Wood, who was captured within hours, explained that he joined their escape inadvertently and reluctantly. Seeking $2 million in damages and "just punishment" for all "prison personnel involved in allowing inmates to escape," Wood charged: "Because of extreme fear of being shot to death, I was forced to swim several irrigation canals, attempt to swim a 'raging' Jordan River and expose myself to innumerable bites by many insects. At one point, I heard a volley of shotgun blasts and this completed my anxiety."

A Colorado couple filed separate lawsuits against a Boulder psychotherapist whom they accused of breaking up their marriage. David Smith and

Jane Harris said the therapist was having an affair with Smith, one of her clients, while counseling Harris, another client, not to have sex with him. After Smith divorced Harris, he married the therapist. But Harris said Smith had married the therapist "under duress," claiming that the therapist also pressured Smith into giving up his federal civil service job to go into the roofing business with the therapist's brother. Court documents show that the therapist had been fired from her previous counseling job for engaging in sexual relations and marrying another client, whom she later divorced.

While Walter DeBow of Atlantic City, NJ, was in jail on a minor traffic charge in East St. Louis, IL, another inmate assaulted and permanently disabled him. DeBow sued the city and was awarded $3.5 million in cash. The city was broke and issued bonds to pay off the debt gradually. The city had been making the payments on time, but they weren't enough to pay for the permanently disabled DeBow's care and rehabilitation. Illinois County Court judge Roger Scrivener ruled that DeBow needed the money right away and ordered the city to turn over to him and his family the only asset that could to cover the amount due: it's four-year-old municipal building.

"They don't really want the city hall," said Gary Levin, head of the rehabilitation center where DeBow pays $10,000 a month to stay.

"But on the other hand, it costs money to take care of Walter."

In Oakland, CA, the family of an 89-year-old woman who died in Honolulu said it was suing a mortuary there for dumping garbage in her coffin. When the coffin containing Mimi Goldberg arrived in Oakland, a three-woman orthodox Jewish burial group sent to prepare the body noticed a black garbage bag that had come in the coffin. It contained a dead pig, a banana skin, cigarette butts, and a crumpled newspaper.

The Maryland Court of Appeals ruled that Silvio Figueredo-Torres, 49, could proceed with his $10 million suit against a Bethesda psychologist for malpractice and intentionally inflicting emotional distress; to wit, having an affair with Figueredo-Torres's wife. The psychologist denied having sex with Marsha Figueredo-Torres, 50, during therapy or before she separated from her husband, although he did marry her just after the couple divorced.

Silvio Figueredo-Torres's suit charged the psychologist with demoralizing him by ridiculing him and telling him to stay away from his wife. During therapy, the psychologist called him "a codfish" and said his wife deserved a "fillet." The psychologist told the husband that he had bad breath and was to blame for the couple's problems.

Nancy Cean announced that she was suing Good Samaritan Hospital in Watertown, NY, for $2 million, claiming it lost a 6-by-2-inch piece of her skull that had been temporarily removed to treat an aneurysm. Her attorney, John Cherundolo, contended the hospital misplaced body parts belonging to at least 25 other patients.

A judge in Boulder, CO, ordered a matchmaking service to pay Gregory R. Hoesli $2,888 for pairing him with unsatisfactory female companions for two years. Hoesli complained that he "spent money and wasted time" in "humiliating" experiences with the women sent to him by Successful Singles International.

Injudicious Judges & Lame-Brained Lawyers

Some judges believe that once they put on their robe, they become wiser than everyone else. Instead, they usually come out dumber. As for lawyers, you know what Shakespeare said about them. Put the two groups together and you have the makings of one heck of a farce.

In Bedford, PA, District Justice Charles O. Guyer, 44, pleaded guilty to promising leniency to a 21-year-old man charged with disorderly conduct and public drunkenness if the defendant would allow the judge to shampoo his hair. The man let Guyer give him one wash and rinse. When the judge promised more leniency if the man would get some of his friends to let him wash their hair, the defendant went to the authorities and returned with two undercover state troopers, who let the judge wash their hair, then arrested him. Offering no explanation for his actions, the judge resigned after getting probation and having to forfeit pension benefits earned in 22 years on the bench.

Steven Barker, 31, of Woodbridge, VA, appeared before magistrate J. B. Polson and asked him to issue an arrest warrant against a man who Barker said had threatened him over the phone. Instead, the judge told Barker he knew the man and did not believe he would make such threats. When Barker asked to see another magistrate, Polson punched him in the face, then followed him outside and punched him again, according to a civil rights suit that Barker filed against Polson. The Virginia attorney general's office argued against the suit's validity, claiming that Polson was protected by judicial immunity, since he was acting in a judicial capacity when he punched Barker.

⚖

Coworkers of Dallas County District judge David K. Brooks reported that on several occasions while alone in his office he slammed his head and fists into the walls and once had ripped a sink out of a bathroom wall. Brooks denied that his "eccentricity" affected his judicial ability.

In Phoenix, AZ, U.S. District Court judge Stephen McNamee sentenced John Arthur MacLean, 44, to 37 months for receiving stolen goods after reading MacLean's autobiography, *Secrets of a Superthief*, which he wrote in 1983 while serving time in a Florida prison for burglary.

Fed up with beeping pagers disrupting proceedings, Harris County, TX, District Court judge Joe Kegans detained some 40 people for three hours after a beeper beeped and nobody admitted to being its owner. She ordered bailiffs to lock the courtroom doors and confiscate all beepers in the room. She finally let her captives go after forcing all beeper owners to take an oath that it was not their beeper that disrupted the court.

When Kevin Robinson of Randallstown, MD, fell behind in his court-ordered support for a child he admitted fathering in 1980, Baltimore judge Richard T. Rombro found him in contempt. Even though a 1988 blood test showed that Robinson could not have been the child's father, Judge Rombro said that an order was an order.

In France, Judge Huguette Le Foyer de Costil ruled that a female cast could perform Samuel Beckett's play *Waiting for Godot*, despite the protest of Jerome Lindon, the man designated by French law as guardian of the integrity of the late playwright's works. Lindon insisted that the play is about male characters and would be "deformed" by a female cast. The judge did order that Lindon's objections be read before each performance.

To settle a dispute about whether a confiscated substance was marijuana, Raleigh, NC, Superior Court judge Howard E. Manning ordered the bailiff to get rolling papers and light it up. From the smell, Manning and a detective in the case concluded officially that the substance was marijuana.

Canada's Supreme Court upheld the 1988 acquittal of a man who drove 14 miles to his in-laws' home in the middle of the night, stabbed his mother-in-law to death, and seriously injured his father-in-law. He turned himself in to police, explaining that he had been sleepwalking. A jury acquitted the man of first-degree murder, and the trial judge ruled that he had not been insane at the time of the killing but instead suffered from a sleep disorder.

When the Ellis County, TX, Commissioners' Court rejected a request for a raise from justices of the peace Milton Gallagher of Ennis and Robert Roberts of Italy, their honors reduced most pending traffic fines from $25 to $1.

In Florida, the Third District Court of Appeal ruled that John M. Butler could keep two four-foot alligators as pets in his suburban Miami home. The ruling came two years after Butler had applied for a state permit but was turned down, according to court records, when investigators showed up at his mobile home and "found both alligators in the respondent's bed" and Butler bleeding from gator bites.

In London, Judge Neil Denison suspended the sentence of a man who pleaded guilty to strangling his wife, when the man explained that her constant nagging for 18 years provoked him. The judge also extended the court's sympathy. "You have suffered through no fault of your own a terrible existence for a very long time," he told Bisla Rajinder Singh, 44, suspending his 18-month sentence for manslaughter. "I do not see that sending you to prison is going to do you or your children any good."

After two lower courts ruled that nagging was against the law, the Louisiana Supreme Court decreed that it wasn't. Conceding that Jefferson Parish resident Frank Brewer "tolerated his wife's tongue for nearly forty years," the decision, written by Associate Justice Jack C. Watson, said "a spouse need not be perfect to be free from legal fault." The decision cleared the way for Theresa Brewer to seek alimony.

India's chief election commissioner T. N. Seshan barred political candidates and their parties from using animals as symbols. He explained that the official action was necessary to stop supporters of rival factions from torturing and killing the actual animals representing their opponents.

⚖️

During a probation hearing in Fort Lauderdale, FL, defendant Gordon Meyette, 43, muttered to a bailiff, "If I had a gun, I'd kill that judge." When the bailiff told Broward Circuit Court judge J. Leonard Fleet what Meyette had said, the judge stood up, reached into his robe, and pulled out a .38-caliber revolver.

"There's one bullet in the cylinder," Fleet said to the handcuffed defendant. "Do you want to take your best shot? If you're going to take a shot, you better score, because I don't miss." After the incident, Fleet was transferred from criminal court to civil court.

Oklahoma's Supreme Court rejected an appeal by a man who lost an election for a district judgeship in Texas County. Josh Evans challenged the outcome of the November election, in which his opponent, District Court judge Frank Ogden, got ninety-one percent of the vote—even though he had died that August.

Concerned about increasing incidences of violence in courtrooms in other jurisdictions, judges at Alameda County, CA, Superior Court decided to install bulletproof shields around their benches. The plastic shields, costing $500 each, protected the judges only from the waist down, requiring them to duck to be fully protected. "It's not a complete security system by any means," court officer Ronald Overholt said, "but it's something."

San Diego judge Joseph K. Davis, 44, was granted a lifetime disability pension after he claimed he had suffered stage fright during his nine years on the bench. Davis explained that he required medication to be able to instruct juries and sentence defendants.

After Birmingham, AL, mayor Richard Arrington complained that District Court judge Jack Montgomery was soft on habitual lawbreakers, Montgomery raised a theft suspect's bond to $9 trillion.

Circuit Court judge Jimmy Dean Sloan, 42, of Anniston, AL, was arrested in Providence, RI, on a charge of molesting the 13-year-old grandson of another judge while attending a national conference of family court judges on the problems of child abuse.

In Wheeling, WV, U.S. District Court judge Frederick P. Stamp ordered Ritchie County to upgrade its jail by hiring more correctional officers; building an outdoor basketball court; and installing an indoor exercise area with a stationary bicycle, weight-lifting equipment, and table tennis gear. The judge's twenty-four-page list of required improvements also called for all inmates to receive a dental examination within fourteen days of being admitted to the facility. "*I* don't get that kind of treatment," county commission president Samuel C. Rogers said. He added that the prisoners would be getting "better dental care than eighty percent of the people in Ritchie County."

While a five-woman, one-man jury in Tampa, FL, was deliberating the fate of accused car thief Alfred Pankhurst, Jr., they sent a note to Circuit Court judge William Graybill noting that they were still unable to reach a verdict and asking if court officials could send in an extra tampon for a female juror. The judge refused the request, even though a courtroom reporter volunteered a spare tampon she had in her purse, and both the prosecutor and defense attorney offered to go buy a box of them. Instead, Graybill called the jury in, told them the budget allowed only lunch money, and ordered them to continue deliberating.

Two hours later, they brought in a guilty verdict. Pankhurst, facing 40 years in prison, said he would seek a mistrial, arguing that denying the woman a tampon may have influenced the jury's decision.

⚖️

Noting that rudeness among attorneys had become a serious problem that harms both clients and the court system, a nine-member Committee on Civility recommended that seasoned lawyers take politeness lessons and newcomers to the legal profession pledge to uphold a 38-step code of professional conduct developed by the panel. "We are brothers and sisters in a profession, not a gang fight," said Chief Judge William Bauer, a member of the panel, who accused attorneys of engaging in "Rambo-style" tactics. San Francisco lawyer Melvin Belli scoffed at the panel's recommendation, explaining that it's "like going out in the jungle and teaching orangutans to use a knife and fork."

Before his election to Congress, Alcee Hastings, the former federal judge who defended Yahweh Ben Yahweh in his conspiracy and racketeering trial in Miami, withdrew from the case, pointing out that his client was broke. "His being indigent," Hastings explained, "doesn't mean I have to be indigent."

James Sinclair, who sued the city of Los Angeles, charging police with using excessive force, met his attorney, Michael Friedman, in the County Law Library. There, he pulled a gun and shot him dead, then killed himself. According to witnesses, before Sinclair fired he muttered, "Attorneys have ruined the world. Now is the day of justice."

The Texas Court of Appeals reversed Michael S. Doherty's murder conviction because of what it termed his lawyer's "ineffective assistance." The two most serious errors came when the lawyer was conferring with his client and whispered loud enough for the jury to hear: "You didn't take *all* the money, right?" and "What did you do, hit him over the head first?"

Detroit lawyer Timothy Mucciante was convicted of running a bogus investment scheme to sell condoms to Russia in exchange for chickens.

Alan Schroeder, 57, a Frankfort, IL, attorney charged with selling cocaine to a teenager, had his trial postponed six times during a two-year period because of his claim that he was unable to comprehend the charges against him or assist in his defense—even though he continued his law practice of defending drunk drivers.

Richard Redd, 46, the lawyer for the Baton Rouge, LA, police department, was charged with malfeasance in office for asking exotic dancers and professional escorts to bare their breasts when they applied to him for the $25 licenses the city required for people in their line of work.

Nuts Behind
the Wheel

Cars and crime go together. Sometimes cars are accomplices; other times they're weapons. But remember, they're only steel, glass, and plastic. The driving force that holds these insolent chariots together is the nut behind the wheel.

Los Angeles police investigating a rash of apparently staged high-speed accidents between cars and tractor-trailers charged more than 20 people with running five freeway crash rings to collect insurance money. According to "wreck scripts" found in the suspects' apartments and glove compartments, authorities explained that ringleaders and recruits—usually desperately poor Hispanic immigrants paid as little as $100 to ride in crash cars—would find giant rigs on the city's freeways, pull in front of them, and brake suddenly to cause rear-end collisions.

According to the police in Clifton, NJ, who arrested Daniel Catalano for robbery, auto theft, assault, and resisting arrest, the suspect's crime spree began while he was driving a car stolen the previous day. He left the vehicle and approached a woman getting out of her car and forcibly took the car and drove it about six blocks, where he had an accident with a vehicle occupied by a married couple. When the couple got out of their car to check for damage, Catalano took their car and drove it about four blocks to a park, where it got stuck in the mud. Abandoning the vehicle, he walked to nearby Bloomfield. There he took a bicycle from a female rider and headed back to Clifton, where he was spotted looking into parked cars. Witness Del de Montreux approached the suspect, who told him he had been mugged, then called police, who found Catalano hiding in a storm drain.

⚖

Kenneth Dean Johnson became the first person to have his car seized in Portland, OR, under a 1990 ordinance aimed at stemming drunken driving. Later, Johnson was stopped a second time and lost another car. In the second incident, he showed police a vial of what he said was heroin, which he explained he was using to try to overcome his drunk-driving problem.

Frank R. Gaininy, 29, avoided being tried for manslaughter by paying a $45 fine for negligent driving after he was involved in a traffic accident

115

in which another man was killed. The Maryland Court of Appeals ruled unanimously that the indictment of Gaininy on a vehicular manslaughter charge violated his constitutional protection against double jeopardy, since paying the fine constituted a conviction and, under state law, negligence and manslaughter are similar offenses that would require the same evidence to support a conviction.

Howard County, MD, Circuit Court judge Cornelius F. Sybert, Jr. dismissed a manslaughter charge against Garrick Wesley, 24, because he had already paid a $45 fine for a reckless driving charge in connection with the accident. The judge ruled that prosecuting Wesley on the manslaughter charge would violate the constitutional guarantee against double jeopardy because by paying the fine he was pleading guilty to a lesser but similar charge, for which the punishment was the fine.

Earlier that year, the Maryland Court of Special Appeals overturned the manslaughter conviction of drunk driver John Charles Glasser because he had already paid a $35 fine for going the wrong way on a one-way road. Glasser was issued the citation before his indictment on the manslaughter charge.

⚖

Michael K. Doeschot of Newark, CA, admitted running over Graham Glickfield, but instead of claiming it was an accident, he told police that the victim had paid him to kill him. Noting that the payment was "not a lot of money," police charged Doeschot with first-degree murder.

In New York City, Peter McGowan, 26, was charged with stealing 25 taxis over a 30-day period and using them to pick up fares to support his crack habit. According to police sergeant Nicholas Vreeland, McGowan stole his first cab by pretending that he had a weapon in his pocket. Using one cab, Vreeland said, McGowan posed as a taxi driver and then, pretending that he needed assistance with a flat tire, would wave down another cab driver. When the driver would leave his cab to help, McGowan would jump in the new cab and drive away, leaving the driver stranded with the old cab.

New Castle County, DE, police charged Timothy Heverin, 29, with trying to get help after he fell out of his wheelchair by firing a shotgun. Police spokesperson Vincent G. Kowal described Heverin as being "extremely intoxicated" when he tumbled from his wheelchair and landed on the street. Five cars stopped to offer assistance, but Heverin fired at them, hitting two.

After receiving reports of a small truck driving recklessly across lawns in Glen Burnie, MD, police gave chase. For nearly two hours, as many as 46 police cars pursued the Ford Ranger, which stopped only once—at Baltimore's Harbor Tunnel to pay the $1 toll.

Westboro, MA, police chasing two men in a stolen car caught and arrested them when the driver stopped to pick up a toll ticket at the Massachusetts Turnpike toll booth. While the suspects were stopped, Sergeant Alan Gordon drove through an open toll-both lane and blocked the stolen vehicle from the front while another cruiser blocked it from the rear.

Authorities arrested Victoria A. Alingog, 31, in Alamorgordo, NM, after she ran a border patrol checkpoint and led police on a 30-mile chase. She was stopped once but drove off again, almost running over an officer, who fired three shots at her vehicle. When she was finally stopped by a police roadblock, she explained that she ran the checkpoint in the first place because she didn't want to get in trouble for having an expired driver's license.

After someone broke into a warehouse in Bridgeport, CT, word spread that it was filled with motorized golf carts. People in the neighborhood stole between 50 and 100 of the carts, then used them for a demolition derby on city streets, according to police sergeant John Carraro. They "all went and got one," he said. "They were doing crash-mobiles into cars going down the street."

When California Highway Patrol officer Steven Cortes tried to stop Randall Marlow, 20, for some minor equipment deficiencies on his motorcycle, Marlow sped off. After weaving through Los Angeles traffic to avoid Cortes, he discarded his bike at Valencia Golf Course and took off across the links in a golf cart. Cortes commandeered another golf cart and continued the chase. "The golf carts only go about 5 miles per hour," Cortes said, "but it beats running."

Despite three convictions for drunk driving, including, authorities said, the time he "happened to drive through a building" and the 120-day suspension of his driver's license, Clayton County, GA, high school driver ed teacher David Ernest Premont, 34, was permitted to continue teaching at Forest Park High School. Principal Margaret Manos called Premont "an exceptional person who commands a lot of respect from our students," but conceded that her decision was based on the lack of other certified teachers and having "not another soul to turn to."

Police in Huntington, IN, arrested William Hardacre, 40, after they spotted him driving home in a forklift carrying 30 cases of beer reported missing from a beverage company.

Thinking he was at a Burger King in St. Louis, Thomas Hall, 38, drove up to an intercom window and tried to place an order. He was actually at a police station, and the booking clerk staffing the window booked him for drunken driving.

Police in Keene, TX, arrested Alvin Owens Bray, 45, after he drove his pickup truck through the lobby of the First State Bank. The bank president said that Bray told him he had $7 million on him and wanted to know, "Is this the drive-through?"

In Morristown, TN, funeral workers bringing a body to Humana Hospital to be pronounced officially dead, pulled up and hopped out to talk to hospital officials. When they returned to find their hearse gone, they called police. Police spotted the hearse, but it led them on a seven-minute chase before they caught it and arrested James Edward Conner, 22. He explained that he stole

the hearse because he needed a ride to Knoxville. But he didn't know there was a body in it.
"I don't know how he couldn't have," said police
detective Dale Pendland. "We thought we could
charge him with kidnapping, but we couldn't."

New York City police arrested Albert Simon, 28,
for shooting his car after it broke down in traffic. "One man opened the hood and began to
tinker," said transit police officer James Hilbert,
who saw the car sputter to a stop. "The other
guy pulled out a gun and fired four rounds into
the windshield."

When tourists in the Swiss resort of Zermatt
complained that many of the town's 370 electric-
powered cars and carts were exceeding the 12-
mph speed limit, police said they would issue
tickets but were unable to find a traffic radar
able to measure such slow speeds.

While warming up his car in Anchorage, AK,
Gailen Byland, 35, bumped the steering wheel,
causing the gun he was wearing to cock. When
he tried to take it out of the holster to uncock
it, the gun fired, wounding him in the buttocks.

Determined to see their newborn niece in central Kentucky, two 11-year-old girls in West Virginia secretly borrowed their grandfather's Dodge Aries, piled clothes on the front seat so they could see over the steering wheel, and packed soft drinks, snacks, and an atlas. They made the 10-hour drive to Harrodsburg without incident, even though, according to Mercer County juvenile caseworker Michael Ray, "neither one of them had ever driven a car before."

A 26-year-old man was leaving the Ramsey County, MN, jail after spending 38 days awaiting trial for petty theft, when he found an empty police van left running less than 100 feet from the entrance. He jumped in the van and started to take off. A nearby police officer shot out two of the tires, but the van sped off. Pursuing police shot out a third tire during the four-mile chase before forcing the van to stop. According to Deputy Chief Ted Brown, "He was trying to run the police off the road when they slowed him down. After they stopped him, he was trying to accelerate and move the police car in front of him. An officer had to break a window to get the guy out." Brown added that the man "was either crazy or had a lot of guts."

Denver police arrested Diane Bedrin, 30, for stealing a fire truck from in front of her apartment building while the crew was inside giving emergency first aid. She explained that she moved the truck when she saw it parked outside because she thought it already had been stolen and wanted to hide it from the thieves.

British authorities arrested Philip Maton after the 19-year-old soldier took a 50-ton tank home and drove across two counties to show it to his mother in Basingstoke, England.

When police stopped a motorist for driving too slowly on the M25 highway that circles London, the motorist asked if he was anywhere near Durham—over 300 miles away. The driver had set out from Kent 10 hours earlier and did not realize he had been driving in a circle.

In a San Jose, CA, court, Sherman Hill protested unsuccessfully that his dog Queenie should count as a passenger in a designated car-pool lane because it watched for cars and warned its master. Hill, who said his eyesight was failing, argued that he was training the dog as a "seeing-eye driver."

In Concord, CA, commuters mutinied against their bus driver, fighting him for control of the bus after they saw him acting erratically. Passengers said driver Kenneth Webb sped through the streets, ran a stop sign, and narrowly missed hitting a pedestrian. He was also accused of punching a 28-year-old passenger and breaking his jaw, after the man tried to wrestle Webb out of the driver's seat.

In Baton Rouge, LA, police officer Larry Lewis had just pulled into the police station parking lot when he saw a 1972 Chevrolet Impala heading down the highway at about 30 miles per hour—backward. He followed it and arrested Daniel Smith and Louis Reed, both 27, after they backed into a service station for gas in the car, which had been reported stolen and had no forward gears.

In the Los Angeles suburb of Canoga Park, John A. Anderson, 72, was picking up an examiner to take his driving test when the car lurched forward. It crashed through the wall of the Department of Motor Vehicles building, careened through the counter area, and came to rest 30 feet inside the building—but not before sending some 60 people scrambling, injuring six office workers, and causing $40,000 worth of damage.

After Fairfax County, VA, police stopped Earl R. Meyer, 51, for going 61 mph in a thirty-five mph zone, Officer Warren Carmichael asked for Meyer's license. Then the officer got a call on his portable radio alerting him that there had been a bank robbery nearby. Carmichael returned Meyer's license without issuing a ticket and was heading back to his patrol car to respond to the call when he heard the suspect's description—which fit Meyer perfectly. Meyer was charged with robbery and felony use of a firearm—and was ticketed for the speeding charge.

After hitting a pedestrian in his pickup truck, a 20-year-old Columbus, OH, man reportedly drove a mile to a car wash to clean off the victim's blood. When he got there, he found the body, which police said had got caught on the vehicle and fallen off when the car stopped at the car wash.

In New York City, transit police arrested Aundray Burns, 26, for trying to steal a well-marked transit police car—with a uniformed officer seated in it. The officer, Daniel Daly, who was waiting for his partner with the car running, said the intruder jumped into the driver's seat beside him and shouted, "I gotta go! I gotta go!"

Before the suspect could put the car in gear and go, Daly subdued him with the help of a passing bicyclist.

After leading Los Angeles police on a high-speed car chase, David Martinez crashed into a building. Arresting officers said that they found Martinez eating pieces of the shattered windshield.

Police charged a 49-year-old man with unlawful possession of a rodent when he drove into Ashfield, MA, with a live gray squirrel tied to his windshield wiper.

After drivers using cellular phones reported a man firing shots from his car on Interstate 95 outside Bangor, MN, police arrested James Hartman, 41. They said they thought they were dealing with a "nutburger" until Hartman identified himself as a Methodist minister from Maryland. He explained he thought it was OK to shoot his shotgun along the highway in the "wilds of Maine" and said he didn't realize there could be houses nearby. "It happens sometimes," said district game warden Pat Devlin. "People come up from a city and they think Maine is a backwoods, wild, lawless place."

In Stockton, CA, Khai Lak, 20, jumped on the running board of a van and tried to rob driver James Moss, 30. According to police lieutenant Andy Jackson, Moss reacted by hitting the accelerator and ramming his van through a brick wall, crushing Lak to death.

In St. Paul, MN, Yer Song Moua, 28, was giving his sister-in-law Pang Xiong, 30, driving lessons when two men blocked their path and demanded money. One of the robbers tried to intimidate his victims by jumping on their station wagon, but Moua took the wheel and sped off to the nearest police station. When the car pulled into the parking lot, Officer R. J. Ward heard the family's yells for help and found the suspect clinging to the car roof.

Odd Crimes and
Odder Criminals

Crimes are not normal. They run the gamut from the absurd to the ridiculous. So do their perpetrators. The following cases typify the atypical ways people break the law—and they provide insight into the true criminal mind, which probably isn't that terrible a thing to waste.

State police shot and killed Rolf Rahn when he emerged from his home in Genoa, NY, after a 16-hour standoff that began when he shot a plumber who was working on his well. During the standoff, Rahn announced to police that he was an alien of superior intelligence who was waiting for a spaceship. After the siege, police found the remains of 49 cats and one rabbit in Rahn's freezer, all neatly stacked and labeled in freezer bags.

"The thing that struck me was how neat it all was," animal control officer Marty Milliman said, noting that the labels not only gave the date of death and time of freezing, but also showed that several of the cats and kittens had been cooked in the oven or heated on heating pads to make them "pliable" enough for freezing. Two labels said demons killed the cats. One indicated Rahn injected the cat with rubbing alchohol because it was "lying on the floor too much."

The Reverend Roy A. Yanke, 37, pastor of Covenant Alliance Church in Beverly Hills, MI, pleaded guilty to robbing fourteen banks of $47,000. Investigators said Yanke told them he spent the money on prostitutes to satisfy his "tremendous appetite for sex."

According to Atlanta police, after James Joseph Downes, 24, robbed a bank in Peachtree City, GA, he had regrets and tried to give back most of the money by mailing in money orders. After reimbursing the bank for three-quarters of the stolen cash, Downes turned himself in. FBI agent Pat Johnson said it was the first time he'd "seen a guy send the money back before he was caught."

Police in McDonald, OH, charged a 38-year-old substitute teacher with endangering children, after a teenager told authorities that youths volunteered to be strapped to a cross or bound to a chair in the man's home and jolted with electricity. Police confiscated 232 photographs of boys being shocked.

Orange County, FL, sheriff's deputies arrested a professional clown for refusing to remove her red plastic nose at a roadblock. Nancy Cherrington, known professionally as Stinko the Clown, was charged with breaking a law against "wearing a mask or hood in public."

After *The Deseret News* ran a story about three Salt Lake City women receiving large envelopes that contained their bras and panties, 11 more women called police to report receiving similar packages, including one who said she got five of her items along with $12 and a note telling her the money was to cover other underwear the thief wanted to keep. The women didn't know they had been burglarized until they received the packages in the mail. The police also heard from a man who received a package containing $10 and a note from the thief explaining he couldn't find any women's underwear in the house, so he stole a *Playboy* magazine.

Jefferson, Parish, LA, sheriff's deputies, posing as Domino's deliverymen, nabbed a 33-year-old man for buying stacks of pizza at a time, paying with stolen checks, then reselling the hot pizzas to his neighbors. Domino's officials estimated that the scam, pulled over several weeks before the manager caught on, cost the company more than $700 in pizza.

In Boynton Beach, FL, Mary Grieco, 48; her 15-year-old daughter Ann; and the daughter's sometime-boyfriend, Melvin Steele, 19, confessed to police that they shot Joe Grieco, 52, to death. They said he was a miserable, grouchy man who spent most of his life lying on the couch watching television. Ann Grieco explained that she and her mother decided to kill him as a last resort only because her parents couldn't afford a divorce.

⚖

After spotting a couple walking down the street in 1992, stopping every few yards and embracing passionately, New Orleans police watched them more closely, then arrested them for robbing parking meters. They said that Donald Simmons, 53, a locksmith, would use a key he made to open each double meter, then slip the money to Cheryl Collins, 38, who put it in a bag under her skirt. Each stop took 12 seconds, police lieutenant Frank Ben said, explaining that Simmons "had been doing it since 1985."

In Los Angeles, Roy Koutsky, 25, blasted the walls of his house with at least 73 shotgun blasts during a four-hour standoff with police before surrendering peacefully. "He just said he was shooting through his house," police sergeant Pat Findley said, "and he didn't see any reason why he couldn't do it."

Police arrested Chante Fernandez, 24, of Elizabeth, NJ, for keeping her five-year-old daughter locked in a car trunk at a shopping mall while she went to work as a sales clerk. According to Woodbridge patrolman Robert Rigby, who discovered the girl, Fernandez said she had been locking her child inside the car every weekend for a month for as long as eight hours because "she had no one to baby-sit for her and she needed the job. She couldn't understand why we were there and why we were arresting her. She thought there was nothing wrong [with keeping the child in the trunk]."

Police in Bangkok charged Julio Cesar de Monraes Barros with robbing several jewelry shops in the Thai capital by sucking the gems through a hole in his finger. They said he had a 0.6-inch-diameter tube inserted into his right arm, running from the tip of his finger to his armpit. A small pump, activated when his muscles were flexed, was then used to suck diamonds through his finger and up to his armpit. Police explained that while an accomplice distracted the clerk, de Monraes Barros would "vacuum up as many loose diamonds as possible."

Police in Omaha, NE, charged a 35-year-old woman with stabbing her 20-year-old daughter on Mother's Day, during a heated argument over which one of them was the better mother.

In Spokane, WA, police arrested Charles Hubbard, 44, after he fired seven shots into his son's computer. "He appeared to be upset because his son was unemployed and all he did was mess with that 'stupid computer,'" said Sergeant Al Odenthal. He explained that Hubbard was charged with assault, not for shooting the computer but for pointing his gun at his son. "I'm not sure if it's against the law to shoot property in your own home."

When Richard Snyder of Roseville, CA, returned from his honeymoon, he found his 1962 flatbed truck missing. He also found a letter at the post office telling him where the truck was. The thief had rewired the running lights, fixed a headlight, changed the motor oil, and adjusted the clutch and a door, but Snyder said he still wanted the thief found and prosecuted.

In 1985, Ed Lopes, pastor of the First Baptist Church in West Richland, WA, confessed to his congregation that he was an ex-convict who had been a Mafia hit man who killed 28 people. His stunned flock forgave him, and he stayed on.

Six years later, he returned to the pulpit to confess that his previous confession was a lie. He actually was a fugitive wanted in Illinois for violating terms of his parole from prison, where he had served time for murdering his wife and leaving his girlfriend for dead. He was also a suspect in another woman's death in Brockton, MA. He explained that he had made up the Mafia story because he thought people would react to it more sympathetically.

⚖️

Police in Oxnard, CA, arrested Leslie Hayes, 35, after he entered a restaurant, fired three shots into the ceiling, ordered employees and customers out, and then sat down to eat. He spent three hours helping himself to pizza, beer, and wine before surrendering to police.

Authorities in Augusta, MN, discovered that two men had been living in a crawl space above the third-floor ceiling of the state library for two months. They used mailbags for hammocks and took food from employee refrigerators after hours, leaving apologetic notes, according to security chief Donald Suitter. Avoiding alarms and motion detectors, the men also managed to steal a television, a VCR, a fan, coffee cups, and steak knives.

A memo from cafeteria managers in the Treasury Department building, which houses the Internal Revenue Service, indicated that out of 2,040 individual pieces of silverware just purchased, 1,430 were missing and presumed stolen.

Police in Hicksville, NY, arrested Ruben Caro, 32, for trying to shoplift two lovebirds from a pet store by stuffing the $90 birds down his jeans. Store employees were alerted when they heard the pants chirping.

A jury in Painesville, OH, found Van W. Patterson, 23, dubbed the "BVD bandit," guilty of breaking into homes, fondling sleeping men, and cutting off their underwear. Victims testified that they awoke to find their briefs and jeans slit across the groin, exposing their genitals. One of them said that he'd slept on the couch after an argument with his wife, who threatened to castrate him, and when he awoke and noticed his pants and underwear were cut, he assumed she had done it.

In a similar case, police in Lincoln, NE, said the arrest of a 37-year-old man ended a three-year wave of underwear thefts. In 24 instances, apartments were broken into and only underwear was taken. Underwear was also reported stolen from eight apartment laundry rooms.

Clerks at a Victoria's Secret store in Santa Barbara, CA, said that when they turned to wait on other customers, a woman in the store made off with 500 pairs of panties, sizes medium and large, worth $5,000.

⚖

Police in Woonsocket, RI, investigating the death of Tammy Petrin, 21, accused her husband Ronald Harnois, 41, of bigamy. They explained that while courting Petrin two years earlier, Harnois called himself Roland and claimed it was his twin brother Ronald who was married to Joanne Harnois. Petrin didn't find out the truth until she and Harnois had been married for two months. After that, the three became close friends, often bowling together. Joanne Harnois didn't discover Ronald's other relationship until police charged him with trying to kill Joanne by attaching six pipe bombs to her car. Petrin had agreed to testify against him in the bombing case just before her murder.

Milwaukee police arrested Gary Arthur Medrow, 47, for telephoning a woman and asking her to carry another person around a room. Medrow had more than 30 arrests over a 23-year period for similar offenses, managing to persuade cheerleaders, motel workers, business executives, and others to carry people. He explained that he made the calls because he was lonely.

Police in Mexico City arrested five men accused of robbing banks, shops, and trucks of $300,000 by dressing as sexy women. Police explained that the leaders of the gang, Carlos Rodriguez Garcia (known as Carol) and Pablo Flores (Pamela), would flirt with bank tellers and shopkeepers before pulling guns or knives from handbags.

In Bastrop, LA, Baptist minister Freddie R. Armstrong, 45, was charged with killing and cutting off the head of retired Methodist minister Fred L. Neal, 81, at a funeral home.

Dallas police reported that someone stole twenty-five homing pigeons from Dennis Donald Smith. "This doesn't make any sense," said the owner of the trained birds. "The first chance they get, those birds are going to come straight back here."

Police in Harrison City, PA, arrested Joseph Fallat, Sr., 61, for the murder of his wife. Fallat explained that he stabbed her 219 times because of the way she placed food in the refrigerator. "He told me he killed his wife," said Patrolman John Simcoviak. "He said she would stack the refrigerator full of vegetables, hiding the milk, and he wasn't going to take that anymore."

Lorne and Cassandra Cooper abandoned their 11-year-old daughter along a rural Virginia highway "with no shoes, a blanket, a couple of Bibles, and some of the mother's journals," according to State Trooper D. P. Whittemore, because she wouldn't join them in committing suicide. He explained that the girl, her five-year-old brother, her mother, and her stepfather were returning from a visit with Cassandra Cooper's aunt and uncle at New Heritage USA, the South Carolina resort founded by convicted evangelist Jim Bakker. The parents began talking about a suicide pact and asked the daughter "if she would go with them to heaven but she said no," Whittemore explained. "Then they asked the little boy if he wanted to go with the sister or go with them to heaven." When the boy told them he wanted to go with them, "they put the little girl out on the side of the road on the interstate."

After a minister driving by rescued the girl, police apprehended the Coopers 60 miles away.

At a hearing before their trial, Sharon Powers, Cassandra Cooper's aunt, testified that the Coopers told her they had been fasting and praying all week and "they had made a new discovery and they wanted to share it with us." They talked for about an hour, although, Powers said, "I couldn't actually tell you what they talked about because what they said didn't make any sense." The Coopers's daughter added that during the trip, her stepfather had been talking about a dog, his grandfather, and singer Eric Clapton's son, all of whom were dead.

Police in Windsor Locks, CT, charged store owner William H. Skinner, 61, and an accomplice with stealing a competitor's dog and holding it hostage to try to force the competitor to close his business.

In New Jersey, bulk-mail advertisers who noticed that their circulars and coupons weren't getting through, notified the authorities. Their investigation prompted charges against 13 postal workers at two post offices accused of dumping more than 10,000 pieces of junk mail, some in the dumpster behind one post office. They accused one letter carrier of trashing 96 percent of the bulk mail he was supposed to deliver. "Some might say," an attorney defending the carriers quipped, "they were actually doing a public service."

Authorities arrested former letter carrier William F. Calkins, 43, after new residents of his former home in Greeley, CO, reported finding a cache of undelivered mail. Postal inspectors said that between the home and Calkins's car, they turned up about 8,000 items, including a $2,900 tax-refund check. Head postal inspector John Freeman explained that Calkins sometimes did not finish his mail route and took the leftover mail home instead of returning it to the post office.

In Dallas, police arrested Robby Doyle Calhoun, 30, for stabbing letter carrier Raymond Bell, 35, in the back while on his appointed rounds. "He didn't like getting bills," Detective Paul Lachnitt explained after Calhoun was charged with attempted murder and assaulting a federal worker. "He told the maintenance man the day before he was going to get the mailman."

Police in Colorado Springs, CO, accused Donald James Brown, 59, a retired grocer, of clipping people's pictures from the newspaper and superimposing their heads on photos from pornographic magazines. They charged that he then sent the pictures to at least thirty-nine of the people photographed, along with threats to kidnap them and make them perform sex acts.

Marc J. P. Cienkowski, 25, of Bensalem, PA, pleaded guilty to shooting Michael J. Klucznik, 31, in the chest with an arrow after the two argued over a game of Monopoly. Police explained, "The defendant wanted to be the car rather than the thimble."

Two months earlier, police in Salt Lake City charged Jerry Lee Robertson, 26, and Cassie J. Robertson, 20, with using a claw hammer to beat roommate Gerald B. Thomas to death after fighting with him over a game of Monopoly.

Police in Peabody, MA, charged a 46-year-old man with slicing another man's penis during an argument over the comparative sizes of their organs in a downtown bar. Police captain J. Stephen Begley said that the dispute climaxed when the victim "exposed himself" and the suspect pulled a knife and slashed at the victim's organ, almost severing it. The victim, said to be in his fifties, went to the hospital, where his penis was surgically reattached.

When police in Milan, Italy, arrested Ettgore Gagliano, 83, for assaulting a Greek Orthodox priest in 1991, it was Gagliano's 59th arrest for that offense. "I don't like priests," he explained. "I shall bash them all until my last breath."

In Minnesota, William Huston, 59, was charged with bigamy. According to a complaint filed by Maria Huston, she met William Huston in the Philippines, where she lived. The couple were married in July 1988 and moved to an apartment in Chaska, near Minneapolis. Maria told police that in March 1989, Huston left the area to find work and returned in April with a woman named Linda, who was also from the Philippines. Huston explained that he and Linda were divorced, but that she was sick with cancer and needed someone to care for her. He said that he was giving Linda the downstairs portion of their apartment, and he told Maria to stay upstairs and Linda to stay downstairs. When he left the apartment, the two women talked to each other, and Maria discovered that Linda was not sick and was still, in fact, married to William Huston. Maria waited six months to file her complaint, and the police took two years to catch up with Huston, nabbing him in March 1992 after he was pulled over for a traffic violation.

In McComb, MS, Melissa L'Anore Bullock, 21, pleaded guilty to bigamy, admitting that she married Truman Fourroux on November 2, then married Michael Shelby Lowe two days later. Her attorney, Bruce Thompson, explained that she only went through with the second marriage because she didn't think the first one was legal.

"Which one of these husbands do you want to keep?" Circuit Court judge Joe N. Pigott asked her.

"Neither one," Bullock replied. "I'm too young to be married."

In Flagstaff, AZ, Matthew Rogers, 24, admitted killing his 20-year-old wife by deliberately shooting her in the head as the couple fled after robbing a convenience store.

Police in Rochester, NY, charged Edwin Coffin, 17, with killing two acquaintances. Sergeant Mark Merklinger said the three were in a car and started arguing. According to a fourth person in the car, when they stopped at a stop sign, Coffin stabbed David R. Steadman Jr., 20, and Natonya Morrison, 18, and then pushed the couple's bodies into the intersection. Merklinger explained that the argument was about the Islam religion, although he said he didn't think any of them were Muslim.

Authorities accused two staff members at New York's Mount Sinai Medical Center of running an unlicensed sperm bank in which they were the only donors. From October 1989 to January

1992, according to the state department of health investigation, medical resident Douglas Moss and center medical school lab director Jerald H. Tedeschi earned $9,000 by selling their semen to four doctors to use to artificially inseminate at least 17 women.

In Gary, IN, Larry Kennedy, 16, killed himself with his father's gun because his family had not let him take a bath for 15 years. The whole family stopped bathing in 1977 after Kennedy's infant sister drowned in a bathtub. Donald Love, principal of West Side High School, described Kennedy as a brilliant student but acknowledged that some students had ridiculed the junior for body odor.

In Santa Ana, CA, June Carter, 69, accused of setting her husband on fire in a dispute over a piece of candy, said she was only trying to scare him when she splashed him with rubbing alcohol and struck a match, telling police "it just went up." Paul Carter, 62, who was hospitalized with third-degree burns, said his wife of 35 years became enraged when he ate a chocolate Easter bunny that she wanted, but she insisted it was only a candy bar.

Police in Aspen, CO, charged Julia Marion Pike, 31, with breaking another woman's nose in the ladies' room of a local bar because of bad manners. Sergeant Leon Murray explained that when the victim asked if anyone in another stall with toilet paper would pass it to her, Pike complained that the woman asked "rudely" and "hadn't said please or thank you." When the woman invited Pike "to talk about it outside the stalls," Pike said she "naturally retaliated" by "head-butting" her between the eyes.

When the bartender at the Midway Cafe in Torrington, CT, refused to serve John Haddon and William Fitch because they had missed the last call, the two men left but returned minutes later with chain saws. They cut the wooden bar in half and cut out part of a staircase railing before police arrived.

A woman in Salt Lake City dialed the 911 emergency line after her husband refused to have sex with her. According to the police report, the husband rejected her advances because he was watching a basketball playoff game between the Utah Jazz and the Los Angeles Clippers. The enraged 27-year-old wife swung at her husband, who deflected the blows while keeping an eye on the close game. The Jazz won, and the woman was taken to the hospital with arm injuries.

In Pekin, IL, Wayne Seelye, 24, was sentenced to six months in jail for biting off part of a man's nose during a fight at a party. A week before he was to begin serving the sentence, police arrested Seelye for knocking a man to the ground during a fight and biting off part of his nose and some mustache hairs.

Los Angeles police charged Jacob Mandel, 18, with burning down two barber shops and vandalizing a third because he didn't like the way they cut his hair.

In Alhambra, CA, police charged Alex Roman Vasquez, 19, with fatally stabbing his father, Alfonso Vasquez, 58. According to Rosalee Rubio, the two argued over the haircut she gave Alex. The father wanted his son's hair long like his own, but the teenager wanted a Marine-style haircut.

Police in Glendale, CA, reported that a man apparently duped more than three dozen women into cutting up their shoes. One woman told them that the man called her and said he was conducting a survey for a shoe company. He asked for her age, address, shoe size, and her favorite styles and brands, then promised her 40 new pairs over the next year if she destroyed her old ones. The woman cut up a $70 pair while the man was on the line. She complained to police after she called a number the man had given her and got Hughes Aircraft Co.

Although her call was the first police had heard of the scam, the aircraft company said it had received about 40 calls from victims that week. Police sergeant Lief Nicolaisen said that the others were probably too embarrassed to call police.

Police in Spokane, WA, arrested a 35-year-old man after finding 100 women's high-heeled shoes in his home. The man had been arrested several years earlier in connection with 162 high-heeled shoes found at his home—and another 500 in a self-storage unit he rented.

Police in Clayton, MO, arrested a 36-year-old dog food salesman and charged him with dropping gallon jugs of wine on the toes of three grocery store workers, then posing as a doctor and trying to rub their feet. Tipped off by store officials who grew suspicious when injury reports kept coming in for wine-bottle–related injuries, police said the suspect would start talking with a store employee, then drop the bottle during the conversation.

Jean Robitaille, 40, drowned shortly after midnight in an 18-foot-deep water hazard at the Cottonwood Golf and Country Club just outside Calgary. The Quebec man and two companions apparently had been traveling across Canada collecting golf balls at various golf courses to resell, according to a spokesperson for the Royal Canadian Mounted Police, who noted that they were outfitted in full scuba gear. "They had weights on and stuff to get them to the bottom," the spokesperson explained. "Being inexperienced and diving at night when the water wasn't all that clear, there is lots of room for error."

Wyoming police arrested a 30-year-old man near the Colorado border with a nine-year-old boy in a car owned by the boy's mother. They said the 6-foot, 200-pound suspect had been living with the boy's family in Wenatchee, WA, for about a year, posing as a female nanny for the family's three young boys.

In Rochester, NY, Carmen Diaz-Vargas, 25, was charged with stabbing her husband Ramon Vargas, 31, in the chest. Police said the assault occurred while the couple was arguing over dead batteries in a videocassette recorder remote control.

Marital bliss turned into a family feud at a wedding in a Los Angeles suburb. Police said the early morning brawl began when two 12-year-olds, one a relative of the bride and the other a relative of the groom, got into a fight and the adults argued over who had started the fight. "When I got there, all of them were going at it. Nearly all 150 of them," said Sargeant Jim Ferris of the Monrovia Police Department, who added that ten of the guests were injured and five were arrested.

Carlos D. Blackston, 25, of Washington, DC, was sentenced to prison after admitting that he knowingly lived in the house of a dead woman and sold her belongings to buy drugs while her body and that of her 8-year-old daughter decomposed upstairs.

A Chinese court in Tianjin sentenced Li Dong and his wife Su Shenfen to prison for abandoning their baby. According to the *Legal Daily*, the doctor who delivered the child identified it as a boy and wrote that sex on the birth certificate. When the parents brought the baby home, however, they discovered it was really a girl. They returned her to the hospital and said they refused to raise her.

Nigerian police arrested 150 people for spreading rumors that sorcerers were stealing men's testicles by shaking hands with their victims. Mobs lynched at least three people accused of the thefts. Testicles reportedly fetch up to $1,000 in the country's thriving fetish market.

When Montezuma County, CO, sheriff Tim Wood found Donald Everson locked in the trunk of his car, the blood-soaked Everson told him he had been put there by a hitchhiker who stabbed him. Under questioning, however, Everson admitted that he had been having financial problems and decided to run away. After his car had a flat tire, he said he hid out in the woods for a while, then decided to try to take his own life by stabbing himself and locking himself in the trunk.

George Juan Kuehme, 20, a worker at a Jack-in-the-Box restaurant in Phoenix, AZ, was convicted for blowing his nose into a police officer's hamburger. Officer Gary Underhill said that he took three bites out of his burger before he noticed "nasal mucus" on his hands.

In Albany, NY, Maurice Jacobs, 34, broke into the Albany Medical Center morgue. After looking around, he taped a note to the wall criticizing the way bodies were being sewn up after autopsies and declaring he could do better. Police had no trouble finding Jacobs, who signed the note, which gave his address and phone number and ended, "I'm open for a job."

Los Angeles police charged a 39-year-old salesman at a North Hollywood glass company, with shooting out 32 store windows with a BB gun. "At first we thought it was a profit motive because he worked at a glass company," Deputy District Attorney James Baker said. "But no, it appears to be more for the thrill of seeing glass shatter and break. He admitted that it was fun to watch the glass fall."

Authorities charged a 27-year-old man with abducting a couple at knifepoint in Picayune, MS. He forced them to drive him to New Orleans, two hours away, where he made them stay in the car and watch a Mardi Gras parade. Then he made them drive back to Picayune. Later he ordered them to drive back to Louisiana. Just outside New Orleans, he robbed them and ran off into the woods.

Jose Maria Espallarga, a private in the Spanish army, was charged with attempting to insult the nation's head of state by sending a letter to his girlfriend. The affront wasn't what he wrote but what he drew on the envelope. According to the charges, "a body with lowered trousers had been added to the picture of King Juan Carlos on the stamp."

British police announced they were seeking a man reportedly seen touching the genitals of a twelve-foot bottle-nose dolphin off the pier at the fishing village of Amble, Northumberland, in what they believe to be the first incident of a sexual assault on a dolphin. "There are several people involved," said marine zoologist Peter Bloom, who has seen injuries on the dolphin's penis that he concluded are the result of people encouraging the animal to use the organ unnaturally. "It's an increasing problem with tame dolphins in the wild. In Dingle Bay (Ireland) a few weeks ago I saw a stark-naked woman running into the sea shouting, 'Come on, Fungie, I love you.' Dolphins bring out the best and the worst in people."

In San Antonio, TX, Rogerio Herrera, 80, pleaded guilty to killing Amelia Perales, 70, his girlfriend of nine years. He told police he beat her to death after she refused to put *on* her clothes.

Mary Sanford, 59, was charged with burning down her home in Albertsville, NY. Police said that after starting the fire she left the house, then returned when firefighters showed up to battle the blaze and tried to stop them. Police reported that she told them that she torched the house because it was dirty.

According to New York City police, a 37-year-old woman and her 13-year-old daughter invited a 19-year-old friend to their apartment, then murdered her and kidnapped her three-month-old son so the older woman could convince her boyfriend it was hers. She was eight months pregnant when her baby was stillborn, and she didn't want to disappoint her boyfriend, who was out of town.

An Australian court sentenced Joseph Taylor, 22, to life imprisonment for locking his 16-year-old brother in the trunk of his car and setting fire to it. Taylor told police he was angry at his brother for coughing persistently.

Warning elderly women not to accept phone calls from a man claiming to be their new physician, police in St. Paul, MN, reported that the man called one woman and explained he needed to examine her over the telephone. He instructed her to disrobe and do several sexually oriented things; then he asked her to put on a light coat, go outside, and expose herself to a colleague in a car as he drove past. The woman told police afterward that she began to suspect something was wrong about the examination procedure when the man drove up in an old car.

New York City police charged Julian Cowell, 23, with fatally stabbing roommate Deborah Bowling, 37, then carving up the body with a power saw. Detectives said Cowell told them he killed the woman with whom he sublet an apartment after she burst into the bathroom and complained he was in the shower too long.

Police in Pocahontas, AR, charged a 21-year-old woman with trying to sell her year-old son. She originally wanted $5,000 but after three days of bargaining with the prospective buyer agreed to settle for $600.

In Westminster, CA, Kevin Vincent Condon, 36, shot himself to death after calling 911 and pinning a sign to the front door of his mobile home that said, "dead body inside, call coroner, attempt suicide." Inside, police found a fresh pot of coffee waiting for them and the victim's body lying on several plastic body bags carefully spread across his bed. A completed death certificate was on top of his nightstand. Police said that Condon, a former mortuary worker who used to pick up bodies from the coroner's office, apparently wanted to make things easy on the officers and coroner's deputies who would be handling his case.

A 28-year-old woman bus driver in Los Angeles reported that two men boarded her bus, pulled handguns, and ordered off-duty driver Germaine Williams to take over the wheel. They took the woman to a back seat, where they forced her to strip, tied her up, and smeared her with tartar sauce. Then they robbed the woman and Williams and fled with the woman's driver's uniform.

When Guns Are Outlawed

Banning guns won't stop people from killing people. When it comes to weaponry, human ingenuity knows no bounds. Anything from roadkill to produce seems fair game when it comes to gaining the edge over your victim. Or defending yourself.

A 52-year-old woman leaving an ice cream parlor in Albany, NY, was accosted by a man who demanded her purse. Instead of handing it over, according to police sergeant Robert Wolfgang, "she struck him repeatedly with a hot fudge sundae she was carrying."

Bossier City, LA, police officer Jim Viola was pursuing a motorcyclist, who turned around at one roadblock, drove around three more, and slowed to drive around Viola's car. Viola stopped the cyclist by throwing a telephone book at him, knocking him into a ditch. "That's what is called directory assistance," Viola said.

Prince William County, VA, police arrested Douglas Ragland, 34, for robbing a gas station with a banana. Explaining that the suspect wrapped the fruit in a scarf to fool the station attendant into thinking it was a gun, police spokesperson Kim D. Chinn said Ragland was charged with armed robbery and use of a firearm (the banana) to commit a felony.

The day after he was released from prison, where he served two years for robbing a bank with a banana, Nigel Hayward, 27, robbed two more banks by hiding a banana under his shirt and pretending it was a gun. A court in Bristol, England, returned him to prison for six more years.

Karen Lee Joachimi was arrested for robbing a Howard Johnson Motor Lodge in Lake City, FL, with an electric chain saw. It wasn't plugged in.

Troy Brewster, a pizza delivery person, was robbed by two men brandishing a snapping turtle. "That sucker was going to bite me. They put him right in my face," said Brewster, who handed over his money pouch with about $50.

Two years after being kicked in the head by a horse, Melyn Richman, 46, of Skaneateles, NY, painted a sign outside her home calling the horse's owner, neighbor George Wolff, a "sleazy lawyer." When Wolff tried to remove the sign, Richman reportedly rubbed the wet paint brush in his face, then pulled a .38-caliber pistol and threatened him. According to a sheriff's department report, Richman said that Wolff threw her down in the road next to a dead raccoon, which she picked up and hurled at him. "The dead raccoon was my only means of self-defense," Richman said. "I had no choice."

Delaware, OH, police charged Russell D. Schirtzinger, 20, with picking up a dead opossum and throwing it at a car, breaking a headlight. When the driver, Daniel Gladman, stopped and confronted Schirtzinger, he explained that he meant to throw the opossum under the car. He waited at the scene while Gladman went to get police.

Two police officers in Oxnard, CA, reported that while on patrol they encountered a man who came at them wielding a live opossum, "its teeth gnashing alarmingly." The officers apprehended the man after a struggle, during which "the opossum broke free and disappeared into the night."

Investigators in Santa Ana, CA, said that a 63-year-old man who was indicted for murdering his wife in retaliation for an extramarital affair, put her through a slow, painful death by tainting her eyeliner with the toxic chemical selenium.

Police arrested a 27-year-old man for robbing two Detroit-area stores, both times wearing a plaid shirt, a paper bag over his head, and no pants, armed with only a hammer.

A man reported to police in the Chicago suburb of Lombard that another man, whom he had complimented on his tattoo, and an accomplice grabbed him in the bathroom of Bogie's tavern, demanded $20, threatened to "bust" his face, then pulled out a tattoo gun and etched the man's initials into his skin. "This is unusual. We have very few cases of rogue tattooers," said police chief Leon Kutzke. "The tattoo-whatever-you-call-it instrument isn't usually used as a weapon."

Police in Toledo, OH, said that LeRoy Vizneau, 82, strangled his wife Mary Vizneau, 72, when she wouldn't turn down the volume on the television set as he asked and instead "picked up a shoe and began hitting him," according to Detective Dave Noggle. He said that LeRoy Vizneau then covered her with an afghan and went to bed. Before police charged him with murder the next day, they had to take him to the hospital after discovering that he had tried to commit suicide by hitting himself in the head with a hammer.

A bank teller in Reggio Calabria, Italy, told police investigating a robbery that the robber used hypnosis to make her hand over $4,000.

Sheriff's deputies in Piru, CA, arrested a 13-year-old boy they said assaulted his mother by throwing the family's pet chihuahua at her. Neither the victim nor the weapon was hurt, according to sheriff's lieutenant Gary Markley, who commented it was the first chihuahua assault he had seen in his 26 years of law enforcement.

New York City police charged a 74-year-old man with killing his 67-year-old lover by stuffing her into a folding sofa bed.

In West Milton, OH, police charged a 63-year-old man with beating his 60-year-old wife to death with two banjos.

In Brazil, Sao Paulo police commander Manuel Camasa reported a wave of holdups by robbers armed with plastic revolvers. Camasa explained that hard times were forcing robbers to switch to toy guns, which cost about one-tenth of what real revolvers sold for on the black market.

⚖️

In Tempe, AZ, police arrested a 21-year-old man for hitting his roommate in the face with a cat. The force of the blow injured the roommate and killed the cat.

David Tai, 18, accused of murdering three gang members, claimed New York City police forced him to confess by threatening to have a 7-foot boa constrictor bite him. Tai requested that the snake be called as a witness.

⚖️

In Bangalore, India, 20,000 farmers protested the state government by laughing for two hours. When their faces began hurting, they whistled. Police did not intervene, according to Commissioner R. Ramalingam, because "there's no law against laughing."

A Tel Aviv court ordered a 16-year-old girl to stop walking around the house naked after her 80-year-old stepfather complained that she was doing it to try to cause him to have a heart attack so she could inherit his fortune.

In 1985, the chief prosecutor in the southern Italian province of Reggio Calabria issued arrest warrants against eight organized crime figures for the 1972 murder of mobster Emilio Palmara. He was fed alive to a starving hog.

Authorities in Taos County, NM, said that Andrew Casados, 25, a specialized "hotshot" firefighter for the U.S. Forest Service, killed his father-in-law, Albert Martinez, 58, by dousing him with gasoline and setting him on fire. Casados, who confronted Martinez looking for his missing wife, also died in the inferno.

Police in Alexandria, VA, charged a 24-year-old man with stabbing the manager of a restaurant with a fork because he didn't like the coffee.

A British court sentenced Mohammed Jabber, 33, to three years for kidnapping a former Bangladeshi politician in east London in a dispute over a debt, forcing a chili pepper up his rectum, then photographing his suffering.

About the Author

Roland Sweet collects odd-but-true news for his weekly newspaper column. His other books of clippings include *News of the Weird, More News of the Weird* and *Beyond News of the Weird* (compiled with Chuck Shepherd and John J. Kohut), and *Countdown to the Millennium* and *News from the Fringe* (with John J. Kohut).